The British Aerospace Hawk

This British Aerospace Hawk T1A, XX185, from 208 (R) Squadron, RAF Valley, Anglesey, was taken by the author from Bwlch Oerddrws in the Snowdonia National Park, mid-Wales, on Thursday 9 October 2009, at 13:21 hrs. The pilot is the late Flt Lt Adam Sanders RAF, who was tragically killed when the Tornado GR4 he was piloting collided with another Tornado over the Moray Firth, Scotland, near the Beatrice oil and gas field, on Tuesday 3 July 2012.

At the time of this photograph Flt Lt Sanders, then twenty-four, had completed his Advanced Flying Training on the Hawk with 208 (R) Squadron, yet because of his exceptional flying skills and professionalism had been selected to remain with the squadron as a QFI (Qualified Flying Instructor). This was prior to his completing weapons' training with the now disbanded 19 (R) Squadron, also at RAF Valley. After completing his training and instructional tours at RAF Valley, Flt Lt Sanders was posted for front-line training with XV (R) Squadron, the Tornado GR4 OCU (Operational Conversion Unit), at RAF Lossiemouth, in Moray. On completion of the Tornado OCU course Flt Lt Adam Sanders was expected to join the famous Dambusters – 617 Squadron – for his first operational tour (at the time of writing, also at RAF Lossiemouth, but to disband in April 2014, reforming sometime later as the RAF's first F-35 Lightning II squadron). *Canon 40D; 300mm, 1/800 sec at f/7.1, ISO 400. HDR image. (Photo by Michael Leek)*

The British Aerospace Hawk

A visual tribute to the RAF's and Royal Navy's successful fast-jet trainer

Michael Leek

With additional photographic contributions from Iain Common, Graham Farish, Brian Hodgson, Alex Klingelhöller, Jamie Smith and Meirion Williams

Pen & Sword
AVIATION

DEDICATION

In memory of my father
William Eric Leek
4 August 1924–5 November 1999

He took part in Operation Overlord; the D-Day landings in Normandy, France, on 6 June 1944, was present at the liberation of Antwerp, 4 September 1944, and in Hamburg on the surrender of German forces in the city, 3 May 1945.

He was a good friend

In lovely, early spring sunlight on 4 March 2010, Hawk XX174, from 208 (R) Squadron, RAF Valley, Anglesey, approaches Bwlch Oerddrws in Snowdonia, mid-Wales, on a regular training sortie. The aircraft is flying through the flowed, anti-clockwise Machynlleth Loop (more commonly known by amateur photographers of low-flying military aircraft as The Mach Loop). *Canon 40D; 300mm, 1/800 sec at f/7.1, ISO 320. (Photo by Michael Leek)*

First published in Great Britain in 2014 by
Pen & Sword Aviation
an imprint of
Pen & Sword Books Ltd
47 Church Street
Barnsley
South Yorkshire
S70 2AS

ISBN 978 1 78159 294 6

Typeset in Ehrhardt by
Mac Style Ltd, Bridlington, East Yorkshire
Printed and bound in India by Replika Press Pvt. Ltd.

Pen & Sword Books Ltd incorporates the imprints of Pen & Sword Archaeology, Atlas,
Aviation, Battleground, Discovery, Family History, History, Maritime, Military, Naval,
Politics, Railways, Select, Transport, True Crime, Fiction, Frontline Books, Leo Cooper,
Praetorian Press, Seaforth Publishing and Wharncliffe.

For a complete list of Pen & Sword titles please contact
PEN & SWORD BOOKS LIMITED
47 Church Street, Barnsley, South Yorkshire, S70 2AS, England
E-mail: enquiries@pen-and-sword.co.uk
Website: www.pen-and-sword.co.uk

Contents

Acknowledgements 10

Chapter One   Context.. 22

Chapter Two   The British Aerospace Hawk T1, T1A and BAE Systems Hawk T2 38

Chapter Three   In service: the United Kingdom 70

Chapter Four   In service: overseas 90

Chapter Five   The Red Arrows.. 124

Chapter Six   Photographing the Hawk.. 144

Appendix I: Photographer profiles 168

Appendix II: Bibliography and sources.. 220

Index 243

Above: The author's second sighting of a then-new Hawk T2 was when this aircraft came through The Mach Loop in mid-Wales, on 4 March 2010 (his first sighting was when a T2 went through the M6 pass, a few miles from the village of Tebay, in Cumbria). Even from this viewpoint the more angular features of the T2 are evident. *Canon 40D; 320mm, 1/1000 sec at f/5.6, ISO 320. (Photo by Michael Leek)*

Opposite Top: Usually up to two Hawks are given a specially designed colour scheme that is applied for that year's display season. This photo shows the 2007 display Hawk, XX307, going through Cad East, one of the many favoured locations within The Mach Loop for taking photographs of low-flying military aircraft. Because of the risk of bird strikes it is rare for a display aircraft to fly low-level sorties until the display season is over. The late afternoon autumnal light in this photo gives an indication of the time of the year, which was on 23 October. *Canon 40D; 200mm, 1/1000 sec at f/2.8, ISO 200. (Photo by Michael Leek)*

Opposite Bottom: Hawk XX217, 208 (R) Squadron, RAF Valley, flies straight and level through Bwlch Oerddrws, The Mach Loop, on a rare clear and sunny day on 4 June 2009. *Canon 40D; 420 mm, 1/800 sec at f/7.1, ISO 400. (Photo by Michael Leek)*

Acknowledgements

Following publication of my book *Military Low Flying in the United Kingdom*, and a casual conversation with my good friend Patrick Adamson, he suggested I write to my publisher with a proposal for a follow-up book. This I did, but instead of restricting myself to one, I proposed *three* new books – effectively a mini series – one each on the Hawk, Tornado and Harrier aircraft. I am fortunate indeed that my publisher agreed to all! I thank Patrick Adamson for his original suggestion, and for his continued support and encouragement over many years.

Putting together a book like this where others have been invited to contribute is not an easy or straightforward task, as I discovered with my low-flying photography book. A major difficulty will always be getting contributors to understand the need to meet deadlines, even when these deadlines are seemingly so far away from the publication date. However, the stress created is worth it if the images selected are visually interesting, for a variety of different reasons and criteria, in attracting the attention of readers. More importantly, it is hoped that the images selected will contribute to a wider visual historical record of, in this case, the British Aerospace Hawk fast-jet trainer, particularly images created since the introduction of digital photography. In this context I must thank the contributors to this volume: Iain Common, Graham Farish, Brian Hodgson, Alex Klingelhöller, Jamie Smith and Meirion Williams. All are, like me, self-taught amateur photographers. They responded to my invitation with enthusiasm. I am pleased that through this book they have been given the rare opportunity to have their work published, thereby enabling that work to be appreciated by a wider audience.

Of the above, Iain Common, Graham Farish, Jamie Smith and Meirion Williams contributed to my low-flying book, and I hope readers will share with me my pleasure in seeing more of their photography in this book.

Iain is a dedicated low-flying photographer who, over many years, has concentrated exclusively on photographing military aircraft from the hills and mountains of Scotland, particularly from amongst the rolling hills and glens of Perthshire, including Glen Tilt, and the hills overlooking Loch Rannoch and Loch Tummel. Iain's 'claim to fame' is that he took the first photograph in Scotland of a Typhoon flying low-level. Indeed, one of his first low-level Typhoon shots was of the aircraft from 3 Squadron – the first front-line Typhoon squadron – that had a specially painted fin commemorating the squadron's 100th anniversary. This was in early 2012.

Graham is one of a very select band of photographers who I previously described as probably one of the most dedicated low-flying photographers in the UK. This accolade is 'only' because of his commitment to the hobby, which includes travelling many miles to often obscure and remote locations in the often slim chance of capturing an aircraft on camera. In identifying these sometimes remote locations, Graham's extensive and thorough research, followed by prior planning, is impeccable, and, to his credit, he frequently achieves results missed by others.

Jamie, a landscape gardener by profession, who lives not far from Thomas Hardy's beautiful county, is an experienced hill walker. Observing military aircraft at low level from a young age eventually led to an interest in photography. His skills have developed accordingly and now, even with a much reduced RAF, he will explore or search out potentially new locations, even if the landscape or terrain would put many others off – including the author for some locations frequented by Jamie! Jamie is also one of the few amateur military low-flying photographers from the UK who has been successful photographing French military aircraft in their own country. Jamie's first such excursion was in 2012, with Brian Hodgson.

Meirion is the doyen of low-flying photography in mid-Wales, particularly the area known to both aircrew and photographers alike as *The Mach Loop* (also known by some USAF aircrew from RAF Lakenheath and RAF Mildenhall as *The Roundabout*) which is fortunately located a few miles from his home. At one point Meirion was probably known by more aircrew than any other amateur photographer

Making a dramatic approach to pass through Cad West in The Mach Loop is this unidentified Hawk T1 from 208 (R) Squadron, RAF Valley. Taken on a dull and bleak morning, 1 April 2008, the cold, damp air is beginning to causing vapour build-up on the port wing. Vapour trails from the wing tips are also just evident. Note the fuselage strobe light and the acknowledging wave from the student pilot in the front seat. Cad West is part of the imposingly dark and dramatic Cadair Idris mountain in Snowdonia, Wales. *Canon 40D; 300mm, 1/400 sec at f/8.0, ISO 400. (Photo by Michael Leek)*

Above: August 2008 was the 70th anniversary of 19 Squadron being equipped with the Supermarine Spitfire at Duxford, Cambridgeshire – the first squadron to be so equipped. To commemorate the event a Hawk T1, XX184, was specially painted in the colours worn by the squadron's Spitfires during the Battle of Britain in 1940. Here the Hawk is seen on the ramp at RAF Valley at the end of a day's flying, and ready for the following day's sorties. This photo was taken early evening on 22 July 2007. *Canon 40D; 159mm, 1/640 sec at f/5.0, ISO 320. (Photo by Michael Leek)*

Opposite Top: This photo of a 19 (R) Squadron Hawk T1 pulling up and away from a location known as The Exit also shows some of the outstanding beautiful scenery that makes up much of the Snowdonia National Park. Because of the proximity of RAF Valley to Snowdonia, this part of Wales is almost synonymous amongst aviation enthusiasts with low flying by Hawk aircraft. Taken on 19 July 2007. *Canon 350D; 200mm, 1/800 sec at f/8.0, ISO 400. (Photo by Michael Leek)*

Opposite Bottom: On finals into RAF Lossiemouth, Moray, after a sortie in support of the biannual NATO exercise known as Joint Warrior, is this Hawk, XX285, from 100 Squadron, RAF Leeming, North Yorkshire. This view gives a good indication of the graceful curves of the Hawk, if somewhat stumpy, as if the fuselage should have been a few feet longer. This photo was taken on 10 October 2012. *Canon 7D; 107mm, 1/640 sec at f/8.0, ISO 250. (Photo by Michael Leek)*

because he was so often to be found on the hills around Dolgellau, Dinas Mawddwy and Corris. Indeed, Meirion continues to spend more time in the hills of mid-Wales than any other person. He has published extensively on a number of dedicated military aviation websites, and occasionally in military aviation magazines.

Brian Hodgson and Alex Klingelhöller are the 'newcomers', but only insofar as being contributors. Brian has been going into the hills of England, Scotland and Wales for many years (and, with Jamie Smith, has extended his choice of locations by visiting French low-flying areas). I first met Brian on a hill overlooking the M6 motorway in Cumbria. Typically, for many low-flying locations, it was a very wet and windy day – made worse by the fact that there were no aircraft movements. None of his photographs selected for this book have been published before. Brian probably 'qualifies' as one of the most dedicated photographers of low-flying military aircraft in the UK as, like Graham Farish, he has, and will, travel many miles throughout the UK in order to capture an aircraft in a new or unusual location. Also like Graham, he's been going to the hills for longer than most. Brian is also very modest; none of his low-flying photographs have been published before, be it on aviation websites or in the aviation press. Nevertheless, his skills are unquestionable, as demonstrated in this book.

I made contact with Alex through my aviation photography website and we eventually met in person when he and his young family came to Scotland for a holiday, although much of that holiday was spent at the perimeter fences around RAF Lossiemouth. Because Hawks are not regular visitors to Germany, where Alex comes from, the number of his images in this book is small, although his contribution is not insignificant because he is the only person to have seen and captured the Royal Saudi Air Force aerobatic team, who, like the Red Arrows, also use the British Aerospace Hawk.

All contributors have written a short piece about themselves. These 'profiles' are grouped in an appendix at the end of the book, providing readers with a personal insight into how they became interested in photographing military aircraft.

Inevitably for a book such as this there will always be some who will be anonymous, yet still deserving of thanks and appreciation. These include the aircrew and ground crew who indirectly made the photographs in this book possible. The mere fact of being employed by the Ministry of Defence (MoD) and/or the Royal Air Force (RAF) makes naming them potentially problematic, even though none have

done anything that would infringe on their terms and conditions of employment. Compared to earlier years, when there was a spirit of generosity and mutual collaboration, the MoD – and some bureaucrats in the RAF – now sadly want their 'pound of flesh', rather than acknowledge and encourage those who genuinely support the armed services of the United Kingdom and the sacrifices serving personnel make on behalf of the wider population. This, combined with the very real or perceived double-standards operated by some in the RAF, does little to enhance or continue the service's exemplary professionalism of earlier years.

With discretion, some MoD websites have been used to confirm information published elsewhere, although it must be made clear that information on many MoD websites, particularly those for the RAF, are out-of-date (e.g. some squadrons are listed as still being active long after disbandment and aircraft long since retired or withdrawn are still listed as being in service). This means information must be carefully checked and corroborated, usually against non-officially published sources. Nevertheless, I would like to record my thanks to the MoD and their anonymous civil servants who put these websites together. The Internet, whilst not always conclusive, authoritative or reliable, is certainly a bonus when writing so far from specialist libraries and/or museums.

A further collective thanks must go to the publishers of *Air Forces Monthly* from Key Publishing Ltd. Even though lacking in-depth technical descriptions and impartial analysis, *Air Forces Monthly* is the best military aviation magazine currently available in Britain.

Whilst numerous contacts were made from within BAE Systems (MAS Division), including their voluntarily manned Heritage Group, it proved frustratingly impossible to identify and make contact with departments or individuals within this vast company who were willing to assist the author with specific requests for non-classified information. Even published contacts on the company's website proved a frustrating waste of time. This is unfortunate to say the least, particularly as my previous experiences with the former British Aerospace were always positive, helpful and rewarding.

However, there were two exceptions. First, I would like to thank Andrea Kay, senior communications advisor with BAE Systems at Warton, Lancashire, who tried her very best to put me in contact with relevant departments. Sadly we now live in a world where the courtesy of a reply is no longer considered professionally important or necessary, but this

When this photo was taken, from Bwlch Oerddrws, mid-Wales, on 21 July 2008, this Hawk T1, XX169, was part of 19 (R) Squadron, RAF Valley. Two years later it had transferred to RNAS Culdrose, Cornwall, as part of FRADU (Fleet Requirements and Aircraft Direction Unit). From this angle the shape and balanced lines of the Hawk are evident. From a photographer's perspective, particularly on location in Wales, this view shows the Hawk at its best; far more appropriately than seeing the underside at an air show. *Canon 40D; 300mm, 1/1250 sec at f/3.2, ISO 200. (Photo by Michael Leek)*

Above: Demonstrating how relatively close aircraft can get with the right lens and from the right location is this dramatic close-up shot of a Hawk T1 from 208 (R) Squadron, taken on 21 July 2008. Note the elevated position of the backseat, usually occupied by the instructor, providing an almost uninterrupted view ahead. *Canon 40D; 420mm, 1/1600 sec at f/4.0, ISO 250. (Photo by Michael Leek)*

Opposite Top: With a wave from the pilot under instruction, against a backdrop of rocks and summer greens, an unidentified Hawk makes a clean pass through Cad West in Snowdonia on 4 June 2009. The contrast between the hill in the background and the black high-gloss finish of the aircraft demonstrates that in good light, the black finish is indeed high visibility. *Canon 40D; 300mm, 1/500 sec at f/8.0, ISO 320. (Photo by Michael Leek)*

Opposite Bottom: Seen dropping down as it approaches Thirlmere Reservoir in Cumbria is Hawk XX265 from 100 Squadron, RAF Leeming. This was taken from Dunmail Raise on 8 April 2008. *Canon 40D; 300mm, 1/1000 sec at f/2.8, ISO 320. (Photo by Michael Leek)*

observation is in no way a reflection of the very real attempts by Andrea Kay to assist.

Andrea also granted me permission to use BAE Systems photographs that were, unfortunately, already in the public domain (and because they had already been widely published on the Internet and, in some cases, in the aviation press, I chose not to take advantage of this kind offer).

Secondly, I must thank the volunteers who run BAE Systems Heritage Group at Warton for their enthusiastic response. Much of the visual material offered was copied from other sources, usually printed, which meant to reprint from these would seriously impact on quality, besides which the copyright was owned elsewhere (i.e. not by BAE Systems). In the case of my specific requests for Hawk maintenance and operating documentation, this was either not available or, more surprisingly, could not be traced.

For those seeking current and updated information about BAE Systems' profile as a defence company – and this naturally includes the Hawk T2 – their website can be a useful source of *introductory* information for the enthusiast.

The hand-drawn cutaway illustrations of a Hawk T1 were drawn by one of my former students in the late 1980s. This was completed when I was Head of the School of Illustration at the Arts University, Bournemouth. Unfortunately records no longer exist as to the name of this student. Nevertheless, these illustrations together constitute the most detailed cutaway perspective illustrations ever drawn of a British Aerospace Hawk T1, and are published here for the first time. They were produced with the full support and co-operation of the RAF and the then British Aerospace, Hawker-Siddeley division.

The full-colour cutaway of an all-weather Hawk 200 was hand-drawn by Anthony Lawrence, another of my former students from Bournemouth, who, more by accident than design, proved himself to be an exceptionally talented aircraft illustrator. Unfortunately, it has not been possible to trace

him since he graduated. Again, this illustration was completed with the full co-operation of British Aerospace.

I'm grateful for the help afforded me by the staff at Elgin Library. They and their colleagues in Buckie have always been extremely helpful.

Whilst I'm self-taught in terms of digital photography, I must take this opportunity to acknowledge the advice and guidance freely given by Dave Allen, Martin Cole and Graham Farish, particularly in respect of my early days on the hills trying to capture low-flying military aircraft.

I must also record and extend my sincere thanks to Graham Farish for offering to proof read my text, correct any technical errors and for his suggestions for improvements. Regardless of Graham's contribution, any remaining faults, errors or omissions remain mine, for which I can only apologise.

At Pen & Sword, my publisher, I offer my equally sincere thanks to Laura Hirst, the patient aviation print administrator, and Emma Howe, from marketing. Both ladies have been extremely supportive and encouraging – and always friendly. It's a pleasure dealing with them.

Also from Pen & Sword was the late Peter Coles, who sadly died unexpectedly in 2011. Peter was my editor for my book *Military Low Flying in the UK*. He was always supportive and, because of our similar backgrounds, encouraged me to take more than the usual author's involvement in how the book would or could be presented.

Finally, and as previously mentioned, I would like to thank my friend Patrick Adamson. He has no particular interest in military aviation, but his encouragement and support over many years has been much appreciated.

Michael Leek MA MPHIL(RCA) FRSA
September 2012-November 2013
Portknockie, Banffshire, Scotland
www.aviagraphica.co.uk
www.michaelleek.co.uk

The RAF's Red Arrows aerobatic team has a well-deserved reputation for being the finest aerobatic team in the world, though no doubt teams from other countries might dispute this claim. In a classic formation the team are here caught performing in the skies above RAF Fairford, Gloucestershire, on 8 July 2007. *Canon 350D; 140mm, 1/1250sec at f/8.0, ISO 200. (Photo by Michael Leek)*

Above: Although the composition of this shot is rather pleasing, it was more down to good luck than judgement on the part of the photographer. Taken on 7 December 2004, it shows a distant Hawk T1 threading its way through the hills of Perthshire, Scotland, on a fine winter's afternoon. *Canon 300D; 400mm, 1/800 sec at f/6.3, ISO 400. (Photo by Iain Common)*

Opposite Top: For most, underside images of aircraft aren't normally favoured from a low-flying photographic point of view, unless the aircraft are carrying notable or unusual weapons or equipment. In this case it was more than acceptable as Hawk T1, XX325, shows off its 2008 underside display markings, in the form of a large diameter and traditional RAF roundel. This was on 27 July 2008. The pilot is Flt Lt Dave Davies. *Canon 30D; 360mm, 1/640 sec at f/9, ISO 200. (Photo by Graham Farish)*

Opposite Bottom: On an overcast day, 23 July 2008, Hawk XX181, in the markings of 208 (R) Squadron, drops down after passing Cad West in Snowdonia. *Canon 40D; 300mm, 1/1250 sec at f/4.5, ISO 320. (Photo by Michael Leek)*

Chapter One

Context

As of 28 May 2013, in terms of front-line operational aircraft, the RAF of the United Kingdom (UK) has a smaller air force than those of France and Germany, with the Italian air force running close behind in fourth place. The actual numbers are sobering: excluding fast-jet training aircraft or aircraft on order, the RAF have 219 front-line aircraft, the *Armee de l'Air* have 244; the French Marine sixty-two (a total of 308 for the two services); the German *Luftwaffe* 302; and the Italians 197. Since the end of the Second World War, if not earlier, this is unprecedented for the UK, yet because of its overseas commitments the UK has arguably the greatest need for a diverse and flexible defence infrastructure (which includes front-line operational aircraft), than any of the other countries, regardless of their commitments to NATO (North Atlantic Treaty Organization, an intergovernmental military alliance based on the North Atlantic Treaty, signed in April 1949). This state of affairs is a reflection of extreme and ill-considered defence cuts by successive governments, including the present coalition government led by David Cameron.

Discussions and arguments abound as to what the UK needs in terms of sustainable defences. Even its so-called overseas commitments are now being questioned. Political short-term thinking and short-term planning – classic knee-jerk reactions – combined with appalling cost over-runs and poor project management by the MoD over many decades has not served the UK well. This has resulted in one fiasco after another, in some cases evidenced by the unnecessary and avoidable loss of military personnel's lives.

* * *

The sobering reality of the RAF *vis-à-vis* some of our European partners is evidenced by the facts. In October 2013 the RAF had four operational Typhoon squadrons: 6 and 1 at RAF Leuchars (scheduled to close in 2014, with the squadrons moving to RAF Lossiemouth); 3 (F) and XI at RAF Coningsby; and 29 (R) Squadron, the Typhoon OCU (Operational Conversion Unit), also at RAF Coningsby; and 1435 Flight at RAF Mount Pleasant, in the Falkland Islands.

There are five operational Tornado GR4 squadrons: II (AC), IX (B) and 31 Squadrons at RAF Marham; whilst at RAF Lossiemouth there are 12 and 617 Squadrons, and the Tornado OCU; XV (R) Squadron, also at RAF Lossiemouth.

* * *

In the wider context of where the UK stands on the international stage and, indeed, whether it has a future as a lead player, not least considering its influence within the Commonwealth has significantly declined in recent years, questions must be raised about the viability of a self-standing air force. In the context of this book, a much reduced RAF, alongside a Royal Navy (RN) with no front-line, fixed-wing aircraft until the extremely controversial, expensive and still questionable Lockheed Martin F-35 Lightning II enters operational service in 2016 (if then, and with only one aircraft carrier in service), training will be affected adversely, and therefore the need for a large fleet of fast-jet trainers will, as a consequence, be reduced.

Notwithstanding expensive up-grades, the premature reduction of the Tornado GR4 fleet, with 12 (B) Squadron and 617 Squadron to be disbanded in April 2014, reducing the number of operational squadrons to three, plus XV (R) Squadron – the GR4 OCU – a reduced fleet of Typhoon aircraft and an even smaller fleet than originally planned of Lightning IIs (the first RAF squadron to be a reformed 617 Squadron at RAF Marham), it is obvious that the days of the British Aerospace/BAE Systems Hawk T1 are numbered. Whilst the Hawk T2 has a future, it will be on a much smaller scale than its successful predecessor.

However, whilst it was originally planned on retiring the T1 fleet by June 2012, following earlier out-of-service dates, it is thought that the T1 *might* remain in service in the training role until 2020, although this seems unlikely given the recent and seemingly sudden decisions to retire other aircraft earlier than planned. The majority of these announcements regarding the premature retirement of an aircraft type rarely, if ever, take cognizance of the vast amounts of development money spent on *extending* an aircraft's service life.

This clearly demonstrates that photographing low-flying military aircraft against a landlocked backdrop makes for far more visually impressive images than the more common photos taken at air shows and the like. Also apparent is the high visibility of an aircraft in a gloss black finish. In this case Hawk XX245 from 208 (R) Squadron, RAF Valley, makes a gentle climb as it banks to port to go through Bwlch Oerddrws in The Mach Loop, on 21 July 2008. The relatively narrow Bwlch Oerddrws is the highest natural pass in Wales, and its three or four ledges are perfect positions from which to photograph low-flying military aircraft. *Canon 40D; 300mm, 1/800 sec at f/6.3, ISO 200. (Photo by Michael Leek)*

Above: Formation flying is an integral and necessary part of the training of future RAF front-line pilots and this includes formation take-offs and landings. In this photo, taken at RAF Valley on a cold, dull day, 23 February 2010, two Hawks from 19 (R) Squadron are shown just after rotating. *Canon 7D; 70mm, 1/250 sec at f/5.0, ISO 200. (Photo by Michael Leek)*

Opposite Top: In order to bring out the colours and shape of the clouds that form the backdrop, this image is an intentionally grainy HDR (High Dynamic Range) shot of two Hawks on finals into RAF Lossiemouth. These aircraft were taking part in a CQWI (Combined Qualified Weapons Instructor) exercise held on 24 July 2013. *Canon 40D; 400mm, 1/1000 sec at f/14, ISO 320. (Photo by Michael Leek)*

Opposite Bottom: In this photograph the black high-gloss finish is reflecting the beautiful, early evening light on 22 February 2010. This is Hawk XX185 on finals into RAF Valley. This is another HDR image. *Canon 7D; 300mm, 1/400 sec at f/5.6, ISO 320. (Photo by Michael Leek)*

Well-known examples include the RAF's Harrier fleet and the Tornado GR4 fleet.

Indeed, until the introduction of the controversial Lockheed Martin JSF F-35 Lightning II (planned for 2016, but now substantially delayed), the RAF has only two operational fast jets, the Typhoon and the now much reduced Tornado GR4 fleet. The Harrier GR7/GR9 was prematurely retired in December 2010 following publication, in October 2010, of the UK coalition government's *Strategic Defence and Security Review*. The decision to scrap the Harrier was more than likely following earlier petty-mindedness on the part of some senior RAF officers who advocated its retirement in order to deprive the RN of its own fast jets, thereby bringing into question the RN's requirement or need for new aircraft carriers (currently being completed by BAE Systems at Rosyth, on the Firth of Forth, to replace the inadequate Invincible class of what were originally and meaninglessly classified as Through-Deck Cruisers!).

Conversely, a parliamentary question was asked in May 2010 about Hawk T1 aircraft numbers in the training role. In response a minister stated that the RAF had 127 airframes, of which eighty-eight were in the forward fleet and sixty were 'fit-for-purpose' (MoD language). One question these numbers highlight is why so many of the fleet are effectively unserviceable? Is it the age of aircraft or more fundamental in that recent and continuing defence cuts have made such a large fleet of fast-jet trainers superfluous, so there's now no need to ensure that a greater proportion are serviceable?

However, and regardless of when the Hawk T1 will actually be retired, and with an already reduced fleet of fit-for-purpose trainers, it is fitting and appropriate to recognize the contribution this aircraft has made to the training of fast-jet pilots for the RAF and RN over many years. This book is an attempt to provide a predominately visual appreciation of an aircraft that, whilst it might lack the glamour of Jaguars, Harriers, Tornados or Typhoons, is nevertheless still a worthy aircraft – and graceful with it. Furthermore, by the time this book is published, we will be even closer to a situation where the British Aerospace Hawk T1 will be part of aviation history!

* * *

In choosing a title for this book I was at first undecided as to whether to include the prefix *British Aerospace*. It did not take long to accept that this is how the aircraft should be described even if the company is now called BAE Systems. Enthusiasts know, and continue to know, and refer to this aircraft as the *British Aerospace* Hawk. The legacy of the name and the company that was British Aerospace is, and remains, stronger than the current group's clumsy title, which also doesn't roll off the tongue as easily.

It must be emphasized here that this book is *not* a definitive or comprehensive history of the British Aerospace Hawk fast-jet training aircraft. It makes no claims to being anywhere close to being a history of the type (indeed this book makes no claims to being representative of the best of aviation photography either). There are others far more able, knowledgeable and experienced in the writing of detailed studies on the design, development and service history of aircraft, besides which such a study was never the intended purpose when the idea for this book was conceived. With the impending retirement of the Hawk T1 it can only be hoped that authors such as Peter Foster or Tim McLelland will do justice to the Hawk's design, development and service history. What is needed for the Hawk is something akin to Tim McLelland's book on what is probably the definitive history of the Hawker Hunter.

Nevertheless, I do not want to suggest that there are not already some excellent studies on the development of the Hawk. There are two in particular. The first is Arthur Reed's fully illustrated *BAE Hawk; Modern Combat Aircraft 20*, published by Ian Allan Ltd in 1985 (though no longer in print and therefore only available second-hand). Reed has a well-deserved reputation for the quality of his aviation writing, and this book is no exception. It is probably the most authoritative book on the design, development and early service history of the type. It also includes chapters on overseas operators. This book is required reading for those wanting to know far more than the superficial and non-informative articles published in today's aviation magazines.

The second is in magazine format, albeit a substantial magazine format, and that is *World Air Power Journal, Volume 22, Autumn/Fall 1995*, published by Aerospace Publishing Ltd in the UK and by AIRtime Publishing Inc in the USA, in which there is a very detailed technical description and service history to date of the Hawk. This comprehensive and thorough article brings Reed's work forward by a decade, and includes details of all operators. Of particular note are the technical illustrations: a colour cutaway of a Red Arrows' Hawk T1 by the former *Flight International* illustrator, Mike Badrocke; a three-view profile, plan and front view of a USN Goshawk by Chris Davey; and a superb four-page pull-out spread of a full-colour perspective illustration by that outstanding aviation illustrator, the late Keith Fretwell, of a Hawk T1A in the pale grey colours of

Weather and therefore light conditions are extremely variable in the mountains, regardless of what the weather forecasts might predict. Indeed, the weather can change incredibly quickly and suddenly, making preparation necessary before venturing into the hills for possibly hours on end. When this Hawk, XX263, was photographed, conditions were no exception; the day started sunny, but deteriorated in less than a few hours. This was taken from a location known as The Spur, just before Bwlch Oerddrws, but on the opposite side of the valley, on 17 September 2009. In sunlight this location is not good as you would be shooting into the sun. *Canon 40D; 300mm, 1/640 sec at f/3.5, ISO 400. (Photo by Michael Leek)*

Above: All fast-jet pilots in the RAF must fly a minimum number of hours or sorties low level, as this is an essential combat skill. Pilots assigned to the Red Arrows aerobatic team are no exception and they usually complete a number of low-level sorties towards the end of the display season or, if possible, en route to or from an event. In excellent early morning light, contrasting beautifully against a backdrop of a pine forest, is this Red Arrow Hawk, XX244, on a low-level sortie as it heads back to its home base of RAF Scampton, Lincolnshire. It was taken from Bluebell, a hill that lies to the west of Dinas Mawddwy, in mid-Wales, early morning on 20 July 2012. *Nikon D300; 300 mm; 1/1250 sec at f/4.5, ISO 250. (Photo by Jamie Smith)*

Opposite Top: Wearing an earlier colour scheme, these two Red Arrow Hawks are caught soon after taking off from RAF Fairford on 14 July 2007, with XX260 closer to the camera. Note that the pilot of the closer aircraft is concentrating on his position relative to the lead, rather than looking straight ahead. *Canon 350D; 228mm, 1/1000 sec at f/10, ISO 200. (Photo by Michael Leek)*

Opposite Bottom: Captured on a grey, foggy day on 13 September 2008 is Red Arrow Hawk XX237, departing RAF Leuchars, Fife, Scotland. RAF Leuchars will be history by the time this book is published, or soon after, thanks to ill-informed and shortsighted politicians. When it does close, Britain will have only three front-line operational bases, the lowest since the founding of the RAF in April 1918, made worse by the fact that in March 2013 the French Armée de l'Air was, for the first time, larger than the RAF, with the German Luftwaffe catching up fast. *Canon 40D; 200mm, 1/160 sec at f/8.0, ISO 320 (Photo by Michael Leek)*

92 (R) Squadron, RAF Chivenor, from 1994. The final full-colour illustration – uncredited – is another three-view profile, but of a Hawk Mk 208 in the colours of the Royal Malaysian Air Force, in 1995. In addition to these excellent technical illustrations, there are numerous superb full-colour photographs, including cockpit close-ups, and photos of at least one Hawk in the colours of *every* operator (the print quality is excellent). The text was written primarily by John Fricker, another authoritative aviation writer, with support from Jon Lake and David Donald. Because no magazine now published in the UK comes anywhere near the depth and quality of this article, I would advise that anyone interested in the Hawk should include this in their collection, alongside Reed's book.

So, in context, this book is first and foremost a personal visual tribute to the aircraft via the author's and other amateurs' photography, with an emphasis on photographs taken low-level in England, Scotland and Wales (i.e. from within the UK). Indeed, it was because of the author's low-level photographs that he'd taken over a number of years when the idea that a book dedicated to this aircraft might be of interest to a wider audience came about. Within this context this book is different to the norm (whatever that is), and with the retirement of the Hawk T1, this book will no doubt be part of a number of photographic books that celebrate the service life of this aircraft, known to every single fast-jet pilot from the RAF and RN. It was because of the impending retirement of the Hawk T1 that this book was conceived, although now the aircraft has been given something of a temporary reprieve, because of training needs that extend beyond the immediate requirements of the RAF.

It must be emphasized that the photographs in this book have all been taken by amateur photographers. Wherever possible the photographs selected for inclusion have never been published before (except possibly on individuals' websites). None of the photographs reproduced and taken in the UK have been taken as a result of any official, exclusive or preferential access or privileges from or by the MoD, RAF, RN, any other government body, or from any other service users of the Hawk aircraft. In other words, all of the photographs in this book could have been taken by any other aviation photography enthusiast. This is an important consideration as it underpins the concept behind the book. And because no set-ups – sorties in which the photographers were notified *in advance* of where an aircraft was planning to fly – were behind any of the photographs, it was never possible to choose the optimum time to take the photographs. All low-level photographs were achieved by luck in that the photographers were 'in the right place at the right time'. Therefore weather and light conditions frequently, if not always, dictate the final result when it comes to the low-level images. This inevitably means, for a mountain location, that many images reflect the extremely variable weather that prevails in such landscapes.

The text has been written to complement the photographs, not the other way around. This is because this book is about photographs, first and foremost, of the Hawk fast-jet trainer as seen predominately in British skies.

I have a visual arts background, and whilst I have an interest in the design and technological developments of military aircraft, my focus has always been on the visual impact, or otherwise, that, unintentionally on the part of the designer, an aircraft has on the eye (a military aircraft is, after all, designed for a purpose, and not for any aesthetic reasons). Perversely, some aircraft become pleasing by their very ugliness – the McDonnell Douglas F-4 Phantom being considered a classic example amongst enthusiasts – whereas the Hawker Hunter has always been considered a superb example of the aviation designer's art from the outset, and the appreciation of this design quality never diminished throughout its long and distinguished career. Furthermore, the Phantom looked 'cleaner' in its originally intended role, as a USN carrier-borne fighter, but over many years of design developments and up-grades became almost uglier, yet conversely more impressive, attracting a huge following at air shows and on open days. Both aircraft were originally designed for very specific military roles and it was the criteria that underpinned these roles that were foremost in the designers' minds, not the visual impact the aircraft might have with amateur photographers.

Aesthetically the Hawk T1 is a pleasing design; its lines are graceful; its curves gentle and easy on the eye (its Hawker pedigree is undeniable and unmistakeable). It is not, however, in the subjective opinion of the author, a classic. It might be considered a classic in years to come, when one or two might be displayed in museums, and particularly when compared to the current generation of stealth designs.

However, the T1 has the design edge on the T2 in terms of grace and elegance, but the T2 has been, like the T1, Phantom and Hunter, designed for a specific role, or number of roles, and these roles have determined its development and eventual appearance, not least a design outcome influenced by equipment and systems that the aircraft must carry or operate with. This appearance gives the T2 a very functional and purposeful look, which is attractive – if one may use that word – in its own right. Indeed, in

As this Hawk T1A pulls up early from The Mach Loop it dramatically presents an almost perfect plan view for the photographer. This unidentified Hawk, from RAF Valley on Anglesey, was caught on a gloriously sunny afternoon on 25 November 2008. *Canon 40D; 300mm, 1/1400 sec at f/13, ISO 400. (Photo by Michael Leek)*

Above: Compensating for a strong side wind, this Hawk from 208 (R) Squadron is about to touch down at RAF Valley. Taken lying down with the focus locked onto the aircraft, the blurred brown patches are uncut grass. This is an HDR-converted image taken late afternoon on 22 July 2008. *Canon 40D; 280mm, 1/1000 sec at f/5.6, ISO 200. (Photo by Michael Leek)*

Opposite Top: Rotated, and with undercarriage in the process of being retracted, this Hawk T1, XX245, in the markings of 208 (R) Squadron, takes off to give a demonstration to visitors at Kemble airfield, Gloucestershire, on 15 June 2008. This is an HDR image. *Canon 40D; 250mm, 1/250 sec at f/8.0, ISO 250. (Photo by Michael Leek)*

Opposite Bottom: A close-up of the front fuselage of Hawk T1 XX245, from 208 (R) Squadron taking off from Kemble airfield on 15 June 2008. The elevated empty backseat shows the line of sight afforded to the instructor. This is another post-capture HDR-processed image. *Canon 40D; 250mm, 1/250 sec at f/8.0, ISO 250 (Michael Leek)*

comparison, the T2 looks far more fit-for-purpose than the T1. The T2 has a distinctive military 'feel' about it, whereas the T1 looks non-aggressive. To take this visual comparison a stage further, imagine the T2 in the colours of the Red Arrows. I personally doubt the T2 would look as graceful and it would require the abilities of a very skilled designer to come up with a scheme that complements the aircraft's shape in the same way that the current and previous Red Arrows' schemes have complemented the T1.

Because the basis of this book lies with the author's low-flying photography from within the UK, this book is also *not* a comprehensive visual record because there are, for example, few images of Hawks in the service colours of other countries who operate the Hawk. The exceptions are those of Indian and Finnish Hawks photographed when on pre-delivery test flights or during exchange visits respectively. The other exception is the photographs of the Royal Saudi Air Force aerobatic team, when they visited southern Germany in 2011.

It was also hoped to include at least one photograph of every specially painted Hawk in RAF or RN service, but again this has not been possible, even from amongst all of the photographers who have contributed to this book. This omission is in part due to the fact that the majority of the photographers represented in this book did not take up photography until the introduction and application of digital photography.

We must also recognize that in the wider context of modern military aviation photography, with the exception of the Red Arrows (see Chapter Five), the British Aerospace Hawk is not considered a prime subject for aviation photography enthusiasts. This is undoubtedly because the Hawk, at least in RAF and RN service, is not a 'front liner', even if it is the last trainer a fast-jet pilot or weapons system operator, or WSO, will fly (WSO is an RAF aircrew position soon to be redundant once the Tornado GR4 is retired from service, resulting, no doubt, in some frustrated officers with no future flying career opportunities. At the time of writing no new WSOs will be trained, again reducing the need for a large fast-jet trainer fleet). Following their training on the Hawk, pilots, and WSOs returning to flying duties, will eventually go to operational squadrons. For pilots this could be the Tornado or Typhoon, and for WSOs only the Tornado.

For the record, I am not interested in aircraft serial numbers. I know many enthusiasts are, including some of the contributors to this book, and many might well consider the omission of all serial numbers from the text and captions to be a failing, but each to their own. However, for historical reasons, I have endeavoured to record the serial number of all Hawks

shown in these pages, although there are some aircraft that remain unidentified (usually mine).

My primary interest lies in trying to create a visually appealing image that happens to be of an aircraft, and, where possible, showing the environment in which the photograph was taken. Whether I succeed in my aim is for the reader to judge. Those who have been to the hills in the expectation of trying to photograph low-flying military aircraft will know that options or choices for composing a photograph are severely limited by the very nature of the type of photography itself and the subject being photographed. Unless an aircraft does a second pass there are no second chances. Even if an aircraft does complete a second pass the weather and light conditions might have changed and there is also the risk that focus is not achieved or the photographer's panning skills slip. This means that frequently the only option open to a photographer is to try to improve the composition by judicious cropping. In other words, and more often than not in a low-flying photography environment, what you get as an end result is just that. Any photographer who suggests otherwise is not only deluding themselves, but those they try to impress.

Whilst this book is a visual tribute to a particular aircraft, it is inevitable when describing the context that matters relating to government defence policy *vis-à-vis* the current and future operational status of the Hawk are touched upon. A military aircraft, or indeed any other piece of military equipment, cannot be seen in isolation. The opening to this chapter has touched upon some of these wider defence matters because they will eventually determine how much longer we will see the Hawk T1, and its successor, the Hawk T2, in the skies over the UK.

Conversely, amateur photographers are not concerned with defence policy when standing on a cold hillside waiting hopefully for an aircraft to pass below them. Defence matters, particularly the year-on-year cuts, only form part of the conversation when no aircraft are seen – a blank – and politicians and a seemingly 'part-time' RAF are not 'providing' us photographers with exciting opportunities.

I have no desire or wish to return to the Cold War, but from a photographer's perspective, particularly in terms of low-level training in the UK, those were heady days. To paraphrase the motto from 12 (B) Squadron, the RAF in those days 'led the field' when it came to low-level training!

And whilst the British Aerospace Hawk T1 might not be as 'glamorous' as a front-line fast jet, there is no doubt that the Hawk is, and has been, one of the most successful fast-jet trainers in the world, alongside the Northrop T-38. This accolade is unlikely to be beaten.

With the exception of very low cloud in the mountains, which could affect visibility and a pilot's ability to exit an area safely, the weather rarely impinges on low-flying training. Here XX235 from 208 (R) Squadron approaches Cad West against a snow-covered landscape on 24 February 2010. For the photographer such conditions demand appropriate clothing – the snow was lying up to 50cm deep and the temperature was below freezing, so it was no surprise that there were only four of us on the hillside. This is an HDR image. *Canon 7D; 300mm, 1/1000 sec at f7.1, ISO 320. (Photo by Michael Leek)*

Above: In 2006, 208 (R) Squadron celebrated its ninetieth anniversary by painting up Hawk T1A XX205 in a scheme which showed off the squadron colours. The aircraft is seen in the static park of the 2006 Royal International Air Tattoo (RIAT) at RAF Fairford catching the light of the evening sun at the end of the show on 16 July. *Canon 20D; 18mm, 1/200 sec at f/11, ISO 200. (Photo by Brian Hodgson)*

Opposite Top: In 2006 the scheme chosen for the air show season celebrated both a million UK Hawk flying hours and the eighty-fifth anniversary of No. 4 Flying Training School at RAF Valley. Hawk T1 XX159 is seen landing at RAF Fairford after its display at RIAT on 16 July 2006. The other aircraft painted up, XX195, was also present at the show. The pilot is Flt Lt Martin Pert. *Canon 20D; 150mm, 1/500 sec at f/9, ISO 200. (Photo by Brian Hodgson)*

Opposite Bottom: In 2007 100 Squadron, RAF Leeming, celebrated the seventieth anniversary of the founding of the RAF in April 1918 with this specially painted scheme. This aircraft continued to carry this scheme into 2008, when this HDR-processed photograph was taken, showing the aircraft rotating as it departs from RAF Leuchars, Fife, on a damp, foggy day on 13 September. This is one of the colour schemes that works reasonably well, the designer having taken into account the shape of the aircraft. *Canon 40D; 200mm, 1/160 sec at f/14, ISO 500. (Photo by Michael Leek)*

THE BRITISH AEROSPACE HAWK

Chapter Two

The British Aerospace Hawk T1, T1A and BAE Systems Hawk T2

The Hawk T1 and T1A

Typically for a new design, early artists' impressions of what was to become the Hawk T1 showed the characteristics of what the aircraft would eventually look like, but the differences between impression and reality were equally as noticeable once the full-size mock-up was built. The first artist's impression was released in 1970 when the project was known as the HS1182, a designation given by Hawker Siddeley Aviation (HSA), the designers of the concept, and resulted in the Hawk, led by HSA's Gordon Hodson. What was particularly evident in the artist's impression was that this design was not simply a replacement for the Folland Gnat or the Hawker Hunter, the then current fast-jet trainers in the RAF, but that the designers were clearly opting for an aircraft that not only met the RAF's very real need for a replacement fast-jet trainer, but that it could also be deployed in the close support or ground attack role. In other words, an aircraft that was capable of carrying a variety of underwing stores and weapons, thereby making it an attractive proposition for smaller, developing countries who lacked the resources or needs for a sophisticated fighter or bomber.

Following the issue of AST (air staff target) 362 in 1964, where the RAF had identified a future need for a high-performance replacement for the Gnat, and eventually the Hunter too, discussions about a replacement took place between senior staff from HSA and the MoD during the late 1960s. However, and to HSA's credit, the initial design initiatives were very much a private venture, funded by HSA. By early 1970 the MoD/RAF had issued AST 397 which specified a fast-jet trainer with close support capability, almost mirroring HSA's original concept.

There are inevitably compromises to be made throughout the design process of a new aircraft, and the Hawk was no exception. The fuselage design itself was very much influenced by the fact that the RAF's new fast-jet trainer would obviously be a two-seater, in tandem rather than side-by-side, as in the Hunter,

because tandem meant a slimmer, more aerodynamic shape. Placing the back seat – the instructor – in an elevated position ensured he or she had as unrestricted a field of view as possible.

Another consideration that influenced the shape of the fuselage, particularly aft of the cockpit cell, was the engine; its size, dimensions and volume. Initial proposals within HSA were to go for the Rolls-Royce Viper, a turbo-jet engine that entered service with the RAF in 1953 and became significant, albeit with early maintenance problems, in the BAC Jet Provost and the BAe 125, the latter known in RAF service as the Dominie T1 (used to train navigators and weapons systems operators until the type was retired in 2011). Another option was the Adour, a joint development between Rolls-Royce and Turboméca, in France, and used in the Franco-British SEPECAT Jaguar. This was the engine that was eventually selected for the Hawk; to be precise, the Rolls-Royce/Turboméca RT.172-06 Adour Mk 9, 151 turbofan. The current version of this engine in Hawk T1s is the non-afterburning Adour Mk 151-01 low-bypass turbofan (Hawk T2s use the uprated Adour 951). Maintenance commonality with the Jaguar contributed to the decision to use this engine, although the Adour fitted to Hawks is, of course, unreheated. The Red Arrows use the uprated Adour 151A.

The RAF announced in October 1971 that the Hawk had been selected as its next generation fast-jet trainer and weapons training aircraft. The contract for 175 Hawk T1 aircraft was signed in March 1972. Unusually for a new aircraft, HSA did not build any prototypes but went straight from a full-size wooden mock-up to a first production aircraft. This and the next five airframes were used as test aircraft, testing the aircraft itself, and its various systems for the purposes of load trials, in other words, the usual intensive procedures that are followed prior to a new aircraft being accepted into service, be it in a civil or military capacity. Two of these six airframes went to the then RAF Boscombe Down for further in-depth testing and trials under the direction of the Aeroplane and Armament

Hawks from RAF Valley, and elsewhere, frequently train in pairs, and this often includes flying low level, although usually the aircraft are flying in line ahead, as shown here (the notable exceptions being the Red Arrows, who will sometimes fly low level through mountain passes and valleys in line abreast). In this example the lead Hawk has banked hard to starboard as it prepares to navigate through the Cadair Idris pass in Wales. This photo was taken from the east side of the pass on 23 October 2010. *Canon 40D; 300mm, 1/1000 sec at f/5.6, ISO 200. (Photo by Michael Leek)*

Above: RAF Lossiemouth is one of the main stations hosting the bi-annual JOINT WARRIOR exercises. Here Royal Navy Hawk T1A XX301, from RNAS FRADU Culdrose, awaits clearance to join runway 05 for take-off in late afternoon light on 10 October 2012. The Royal Navy is one of the oldest, if not the oldest, military flying operator in the world, pre-dating the RAF by six years. This airframe was formerly part of 208 (R) Squadron at RAF Valley. *Canon 40D; 300mm, 1/800 sec at f/5.6, ISO 400. (Photo by Michael Leek)*

Opposite Top: Returning from a JOINT WARRIOR exercise sortie over the West Coast of Scotland is Royal Navy Hawk T1A XX159, captured on 18 April 2012. *Canon 7D; 200mm, 1/640 sec at f/7.1, ISO 400. (Photo by Michael Leek)*

Opposite Bottom: Royal Navy Hawks taking part in October's JOINT WARRIOR exercise were parked on what was for many years 14 Squadron's ramp at RAF Lossiemouth. As the aircraft were being prepared for the third sortie of the day this Hawk T1A, XX281, went 'technical' – meaning it was not able to fly. Here it's being towed to a hangar, suggesting the problem is more than superficial and cannot be rectified on the ramp. Photo taken on 4 October 2012. *Canon 40D; 73mm, 1/250 sec at f/18, ISO 320. (Photo by Michael Leek)*

Experimental Establishment (A&AEE). The A&AEE was an important government research facility that dealt exclusively with the testing and evaluation of *all* British military aircraft before it was closed and its services subsumed within what became the privatized defence contracting company known as QinetiQ.

Rolled out on 12 August 1974, the first flight of the Hawk T1 took place a few days later on 21 August from HSA's airfield at Dunsfold in Surrey with Hawker Siddeley's Chief Test Pilot Duncan Simpson at the controls. Whilst other HSA divisions built sections of the Hawk it was at Dunsfold that final assembly took place. This continued until 1988 when production was transferred to BAe Warton in Lancashire, following the closure of Dunsfold. BAe – or British Aerospace to give the company its full title – took over or subsumed Hawker Siddeley in 1977, thereby marking the end of yet another autonomous British aviation company.

Just over two years after the first flight the Hawk entered RAF service in late 1976. The first stations to receive the type were No. 4 Flying Training School at RAF Valley for advanced flying training, and RAF Chivenor and RAF Brawdy, for tactical weapons training.

The Hawk 50, the export version of the Hawk T1 designed specifically as a dual-role advanced trainer and lightweight fighter/ground-attack aircraft, first flew in May 1976, though as first produced had limited ground-attack capabilities.

In summary, the manufacturing history of the Hawk is as follows: Hawker Siddeley, 1974-1977; British Aerospace 1977-1999; and BAE Systems (MAS Division) 1999-to date. In 2013 the unit cost of a Hawk T1 for RAF service was over £24 million (it was less than £3 million when the Hawk first flew in 1974). As previously mentioned, 176 T1 aircraft have been delivered. This includes eighty-nine aircraft converted to T1A standards and eighty T1 and T1As that have had their fuselages replaced or upgraded to extend their operational life. Even so, many of the total airframes built remain in storage, begging the question as to the efficacy of such long-term development costs and how accurate the RAF is in predicting actual numbers required as this scenario is not exclusive to the Hawk. Of course, there is also the consideration that because airframes have a finite life, measured in flying hours, reserves are often needed in order to keep a minimum airworthy in order to meet training needs.

* * *

The RN acquired twelve aircraft from the RAF, who used them to replace their Hawker Hunters, though now the RN have fourteen Hawks. Amongst other duties, navy Hawks are used to provide realistic training via simulated attacks on RN and other NATO warships, particularly during Flag Officer Sea Training (FOST) off the coasts of Devon and Cornwall (an obligatory training regime of six weeks' duration that must be completed successfully immediately prior to a warship or auxiliary being deployed operationally). This sea training is colloquially known by the RN and RFA (Royal Fleet Auxiliary) as the 'Thursday war' for the simple reason that that is the usual day it takes place (experienced by the author from the bridge of the RFA *Green Rover* when Hawker Hunters were in service with the RN).

Further primary roles for RN Hawks are through exercises such as the bi-annual JOINT WARRIOR exercises held in northern England and throughout the north west of Scotland, where RN Hawks work alongside Dassault Falcons, with the Hawks simulating anti-ship missile attacks. These situations provide much needed training, in a simulated war environment, for warships' anti-aircraft and anti-missile systems and operators to be tested to the full, the agility of the Hawk proving to be exceptional under such circumstances (as witnessed by the author on a number of occasions over the west coast of Scotland).

JOINT WARRIOR exercises also include Hawks from 100 Squadron, RAF Leeming. Hawks from both the RN and RAF share the role of simulated attacks on warships and auxiliaries, with 100 Squadron also undertaking Dissimilar Air Combat Training with other aircraft, and Close Air Support sorties throughout those parts of Scotland where ground forces are exercising.

* * *

The Red Arrows received their Hawks in 1980 when they retired their Folland Gnats, which they had been flying since 1965 (see Chapter Five). Another unit or organization to receive Hawks during its early service life was the ETPS, or Empire Test Pilots School, based at RAF Boscombe Down. They received three aircraft in 1981 and, once arrived at Boscombe, these were re-painted in the distinctive red, white and blue worn by most, if not all, ETPS aircraft.

As will be clearly obvious from the photographs in this book, Hawks in RAF and RN service are painted a uniform gloss black, the exceptions being anniversary specials or the annual Hawk display aircraft. From a photographer's point of view this is not only boring, but can sometimes make metering difficult for the camera, but then military aircraft are rarely painted to satisfy the enthusiast, at least in the UK, unlike some of our colleagues in NATO. However, there are

On a clear, bright day, the autumn light and resulting warm colours in Snowdonia National Park are stunning, and contrast well with the black-painted Hawks in UK military service, as in this example of Royal Navy Hawk T1A XX224 as it navigates through the Cadair Idris pass on 24 October 2007. Interestingly, and maybe surprisingly, black was determined to be of higher visibility than the former red-and-white colour schemes previously worn by military training aircraft. In many circumstances, particularly low level in the mountains where there is little vegetation, black is not high visibility, at least as seen from the ground! *Canon 40D; 400mm, 1/800 sec at f/5.6, ISO 400. (Photo by Michael Leek)*

Above: Sometimes scale and height are difficult to capture on camera when an aircraft is low level, but in this rare example, taken on a dull, grey day on 17 September 2009 in The Mach Loop, the backdrop of a farm gate gives an indication of the height Hawk pilots fly at as part of their vitally important low-level training. *Canon 40D; 420mm, 1/800 sec at f/4.0, ISO 500. (Photo by Michael Leek)*

Opposite Top: A nice profile view in good light of Hawk T1A XX315, in 19 (R) Squadron markings, passing through the Bwlch Llyn Bach pass in The Mach Loop (also known as the Machynlleth Loop) in Wales on 27 May 2010. The wing hardpoints are present but empty; the Aden 30mm cannon pod (now withdrawn) dominates the underneath of the aircraft. The Hawks from RAF Valley are almost daily visitors to the range at Pembrey in South Wales and are often seen low level en route to or from the range. *Canon 7D; 300mm, 1/800 sec at f/5, ISO 200. (Photo by Brian Hodgson)*

Opposite Bottom: Aggressive manoeuvres to navigate through a pass or glen are not always necessary, suggesting that many are for the benefit of amateur photographers, particularly in popular locations such as mid-Wales, where pilots and instructors are aware that photographers will be on the hillsides. In this shot, of Hawk XX187, the aircraft is passing straight and level through the Cadair Idris pass on 17 September 2009. *Canon 40D; 420mm, 1/800 sec at f/4.0, ISO 500. (Photo by Michael Leek)*

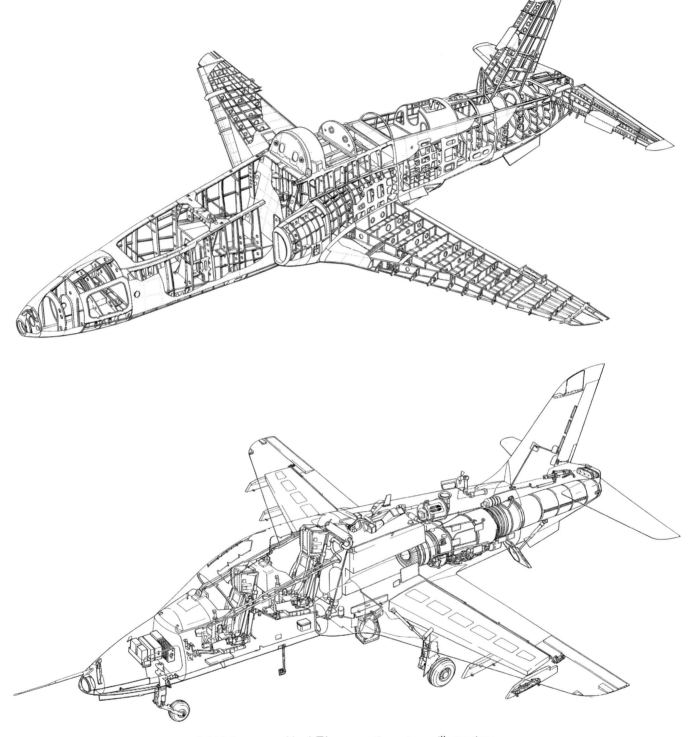

British Aerospace Hawk T1: perspective cutaway illustrations

Above: This perspective line illustration is the most complete illustration to have been published of the structure of a Hawk T1. It shows clearly all fixed components such as frames, stringers, longerons , ribs and bulkheads, etc. For clarity most moving parts such as the rudder, ailerons, flaps, air brakes, etc., have been excluded, as have most access panels. Within the wider context of modern aircraft design there is nothing unusual in the structural design of the Hawk. *(School of Illustration, Arts University Bournemouth, c1994)*

Below: In contrast to the previous illustration, this perspective – using exactly the same viewpoint as before – shows all fittings within a Hawk T1, from avionics in the nose through to cockpit, flying controls, ejection seats, fuel tanks and engine. For clarity all structural elements have been excluded. Comparing the two illustrations gives a clear idea of how the Hawker Siddeley designers had to ensure a rigid and strong structure, yet have sufficient internal space to accommodate the equipment necessary for a fast-jet trainer. One key aspect of the success of the Hawk is that ease of access makes maintenance far less complicated than with many other aircraft. This means turn-around times are fast, thereby enabling a jet to be returned to flying condition relatively quickly. *(School of Illustration, Arts University Bournemouth, c1994)*

With the houses of Bowness-on-Windermere in the background, the Reds, in Five Arrow formation and coloured smoke 'on', head south down Windermere and present a fine view to the thousands of spectators who lined the shore of Windermere that day. There is no doubt that in the UK there is much public pride in the Red Arrows and their presence at an air show probably encourages many more thousands to attend. Photo taken on 24 July 2011. *Canon 7D; 300mm, 1/1000 sec at f/7.1, ISO 250. (Photo by Brian Hodgson)*

Above: 208 (R) Squadron's Hawk T1, XX234, is seen at the RAF Northolt night shoot held on 3 December 2012. XX234 was delivered to the RAF on 22 September 1978. It was flown to RAF Shawbury for storage on 21 July 2011 but its stay was only temporary as it left for MoD Boscombe Down, by road, on 18 October 2012. *Canon 50D; 55mm, 8 secs at f/8, ISO 200. (Photo by Brian Hodgson)*

Opposite Top: Sitting on the ramp between JOINT WARRIOR sorties at RAF Lossiemouth is Hawk T1A XX256, in 208 (R) Squadron colours. This was taken on 4 October 2012, the aircraft having been earlier made ready for its second sortie of the day. *Canon 40D; 33mm, 1/640 sec at f/8.0, ISO 250. (Photo by Michael Leek)*

Opposite Bottom: A front fuselage close-up of Hawk T1A XX256, on the ramp at RAF Lossiemouth, with XV (R) Squadron's Tornado GR4s in the background on 4 October 2012. Again evident is the vision for both student and instructor, which compares significantly with that on the new F-35 Lightning II. Note the standard double-width step ladder, used for all Hawks. *Canon 40D; 61mm, 1/500 sec at f/8.0, ISO 250. (Photo by Michael Leek)*

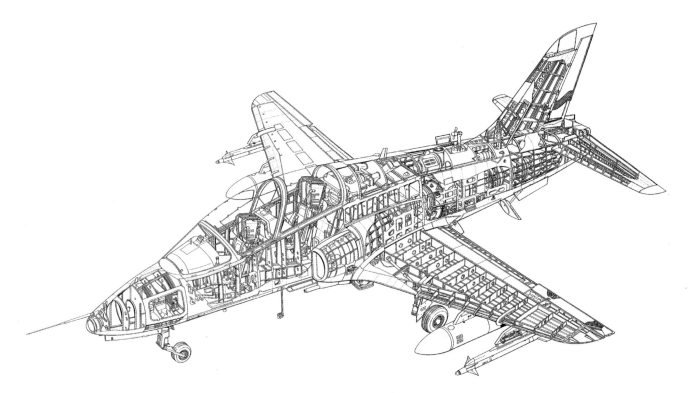

This third perspective line illustration combines the structural illustration with the fittings and equipment illustration, providing an opportunity to see the relationship of one with the other. Collectively, these three illustrations represent the most detailed ever drawn of a Hawk T1 and were produced with the full co-operation of British Aerospace and the RAF. *(School of Illustration, Arts University Bournemouth, c1994)*

supposedly sound reasons for the high-gloss black colour scheme. Back in late 1992 tests were conducted at RAF Chivenor to establish the optimum colour scheme that would make the Hawk highly visible under most conditions, from high to low level. At this point Hawks being used for advanced pilot training were painted in red and white whilst aircraft for weapons training were two-tone camouflaged, later changed to a warm mid-grey. These colour visibility tests, known as Longview 2, had aircraft painted in a variety of schemes, from the then two-tone tactical camouflage, dark grey topsides (almost sea-grey from Second World War days and identical to the grey used on English Electric Lightnings) with light grey undersides (sometimes with a false cockpit canopy painted on the belly), and matt black.

It was eventually deemed that a high-gloss black was the most effective, though the evidence that led to this decision does not seem to be publically available, because visually, the way colour on an object is perceived, the former red-and-white scheme would make the aircraft more visible at a distance and in poor visibility. This can be confirmed when Hawks are low level, for example. It is sometime before an approaching Hawk in gloss black is visible to the naked eye. Against a sky, *most* aircraft, regardless of colour scheme, appear as a silhouette long before detail becomes identifiable.

Technically the Hawk is a low-wing monoplane, constructed using conventional semi-monocoque construction in that the fuselage consists of a combination of bulkheads, frames and formers connected and strengthened by longerons and covered by a skin. The wings have a moderate sweep with a 2 degree dihedral and include trailing-edge slotted flaps. Structurally the wings comprise the now traditional method of two spars, front and rear, between which, and extending to the leading edge, are a number of ribs, each of which is linked through stringers; the whole airframe is covered by a metal skin. The wings contain integral fuel tanks, located between the front and rear spars, inside what is the main wing box. The fin and tailplane – in the aircraft industry more usually referred to collectively as the empennage – are constructed similarly to the wings. The tailplane is one piece and therefore all-moving, with a 10 degree dihedral. Altogether these components provide the strength that enables the aircraft to cope with the many stresses that are inherent when flying.

The structure of a Hawk, including undercarriage, is broken down into sixty components of which the fuselage comprises eighteen; the main wings eleven; the empennage assembly six (including the under rear fuselage airbrake); the nose-wheel assembly four

Hawk T1A XX201 from 208 (R) Squadron, RAF Valley, creates a pleasing contrast with the lush green of summer foliage as it goes through the Cadair Idris pass in mid-Wales, on a mid afternoon on 30 June 2009. It can sometimes be challenging photographing a black aircraft against a light background – the camera's metering system can sometimes get confused, resulting in either the aircraft being under-exposed or the background. From a photography perspective the former red-and-white colour scheme is preferred, but then military aircraft are not painted for the benefit of amateur photographers – with the exception of commemorative or display schemes. *Canon 40D; 300mm, 1/800 sec at f/8.0, ISO 320. (Photo by Michael Leek)*

Above: An early morning pairs landing into RAF Valley by aircraft from 208 (R) Squadron (from left to right; XX187 and XX224), 23 February 2010. *Canon 40D: 300mm, 1/500 sec at f7.1, ISO 125. (Photo by Michael Leek)*

Opposite Top: If visibility is good, low flying in the winter is no problem for the pilots; it's only the photographers who have to suffer – for the sake of their hobby. Here an unidentified Hawk heads through Cad West, part of the Cadair Idris pass, on a very cold morning on 25 February 2010. *Canon 40D; 275mm, 1/320 sec at f8.0, ISO 250. (Photo by Michael Leek)*

Opposite Bottom: Two Royal Navy pilots take their Hawk T1, XX301, from RNAS Culdrose, on a training flight through The Mach Loop on 11 February 2009. *Canon 40D; 300mm, 1/500 sec at f7.1, ISO 500. (Photo by Michael Leek)*

and the main undercarriage six. The balance of fifteen includes various access panels and fairings.

The cockpit 'bubble' is in two parts, a forward fixed curved windscreen, made of stretched acrylic, and a large single-piece canopy that is hinged on the starboard side. Aircrew access is always from the port side, usually by means of a mobile double-width set of steps, as will be evident in some of the photographs in this book. The canopy is divided by a central support, angled towards the rear, with a cross-beam extending across the width to provide strength and rigidity. Within this cross-beam and the aft-leaning support is the fixed instructor's windscreen. Both student pilot (front seat) and the instructor (rear seat) have two rear-view mirrors each.

The crew sit on Martin Baker Mk 10 zero-zero, rocket-assisted ejection seats, which means that the crew can evacuate the aircraft at zero altitude and at zero speed. In other words, the seat is designed to not only operate at a maximum altitude of 15,200 metres (50,000 feet plus), but is also designed to operate successfully when the aircraft is stationary and on the ground. The firing sequence for ejecting is that the instructor ejects first, initiating the sequence. One tenth of a second after the firing handle has been pulled, the miniature detonating cord, or MDC, shatters the rear part of the canopy. A twentieth of a second later the seat ejects through the canopy frame. The front MDC shatters the front top part of the canopy a forty-fifth of a second after the rear firing handle has been pulled, followed, at a fifty-fifth of a second, by the front seat ejecting. Under normal conditions the whole sequence of first shattering the rear part of the canopy to getting both the student and instructor out takes less than a second, though the seats may be ejected independently of each other. Another important survival factor is that the seats eject at a slightly different angle to each other. This is to ensure there is no risk of the seats colliding once they've left the aircraft.

Aft of the cockpit cell's rear pressure bulkhead – the cockpit is fully pressurized – is the fuselage bag fuel tank. Behind this is the engine bay, which extends aft to the jet pipe exhaust, making the overall length of the Hawk as compact as possible. From the cutaway illustrations reproduced here, it will be obvious that the design length of the Hawk's fuselage could not have been made any less. The key factors are the forward undercarriage space, the minimum ergonomic space for the crew, the integral fuselage fuel tank, or bag, the length of the engine and the exhaust jet pipe. And the whole airframe is kept as low as possible to facilitate easy maintenance.

In summary, the Hawk T1 is a conventionally designed and built aircraft, representative of many being built from designs dating back to the 1970s. It has, therefore, nothing unusual about it.

As at July 2013 the Hawk T1's primary role in RAF service is as an advanced fast-jet trainer, with successfully qualified pilots being posted to the Tornado GR4, the Typhoon F2/FGR4 and the fifth generation F-35 Joint Combat Aircraft, the Lightning II, proposed or planned for entry into service in 2016. The RN does not currently have any immediate requirements for fast-jet pilots until the service introduction of the Lightning II. However, some qualified RN pilots, previously trained on the Hawk for operational service on the Harrier until the latter was prematurely retired, are training to fly the Lightning II at Elgin Air Force Base in the USA. In addition to fast-jet training, the Hawk is also used in the final phase training for navigators/weapons systems operators (WSO) selected to fly the Tornado GR4, though this facility is in draw-down as the Tornado fleet has been prematurely reduced, and there is already a surplus of Tornado GR4 WSOs.

The Hawk T1 is used solely as an advanced fast-jet trainer, primarily at RAF Valley, whereas the Hawk T1A is equipped to operational standards in that it can undertake a number of war roles, and therefore carry a significant weapons load. These 'war roles' include air-to-air (air combat), air-to-ground (more commonly known as ground attack), and the all essential and necessary low-flying training. At its most potent, the T1A can carry on its underwing pylons two Sidewinder AIM-9L air-to-air missiles and, until recently, a 30mm Aden cannon in a self-contained pod that was carried under the centre fuselage. Weapons sighting and aiming is through an integrated strike and interception system, supported, if required, by video recorders.

The hourly operational costs of running fast jets is extremely high, not least because of the hidden costs that include forward and depth servicing, fuel, crew and training costs, the cost of capital charge and depreciation (including amortization). The most recently published figures for the Hawk T1 and T1A, via a written parliamentary question and answer in March 2011, are from 2010-2011, and are, on the admission of the Parliamentary Under-Secretary of State for Defence, averages. For the Hawk T1 and T1A from 19 (R), 208 (R) and 100 Squadrons, it was £10,000 (for 2013 this equates to £10,900, and includes simulator and other training infrastructure costs). For RN Hawks it is £7,000 (2013: £7,600), and for the Red Arrows £6,000 (2013: £6,500).

In order to meet its primary role the Hawk has been designed to be highly manoeuvrable. In level flight it can reach Mach 0.8 and Mach 1.5 in a dive, thereby

Hawk T1A XX201, from 208 (R) Squadron, catches the sun and shows off the topside of the 2010 display scheme as it approaches the corner above Tal-y-Llyn lake in The Mach Loop in Wales on 21 October 2010. This was one of two aircraft in this special scheme. Once the air show season is over is often the best time to catch the special colour scheme Hawks low level. By late 2010 the two specially painted Hawks were soon on normal day-to-day flying operations and were often seen in the hills of Wales. The display pilot for the 2010 season was Flt Lt Scott Griffith. *Canon 7D; 300mm, 1/800 sec at f/5 + 1.4 converter, ISO 160. (Photo by Brian Hodgson)*

Above: In general, the schemes used for the Hawk display aircraft are often innovative and sometimes attractive, but in 2005 the scheme chosen did not seem to meet these criteria. It was not popular amongst some enthusiasts and earned the nickname 'Custard Nose'. Perhaps the authorities thought the same, since in February 2006 the only aircraft painted up, Hawk T1, XX309, was put out of sight and into long-term storage at RAF Shawbury, where it was photographed on 21 July 2011. *Canon 50D; 24mm, 1/13 sec at f/4, ISO 400. (Photo by Brian Hodgson)*

Opposite Top: A rare opportunity to capture a Hawk taking off without the usual clutter of hangars and other airfield 'props' to spoil the composition is at Kemble, in Gloucestershire (a former home to the Red Arrows). In this shot Hawk T1A XX284, from 100 Squadron, RAF Leeming, is caught retracting its undercarriage, on 15 June 2008. *Canon 40D; 200mm, 1/1250 sec at f/9.0, ISO 400. (Photo by Michael Leek)*

Opposite Bottom: With Raven Crag forming the backdrop, 100 Squadron Hawk T1A XX289, forming part of a flight of two aircraft, is seen heading north over Thirlmere Reservoir on 11 May 2006. 100 Squadron converted from the Canberra to the Hawk at RAF Wyton in 1991 before moving to RAF Finningley in 1994. With the closure of RAF Finningley in 1996, the squadron was on the move again, this time to RAF Leeming, where it still resides. *Canon 30D; 300mm, 1/640 sec at f/7.1, ISO 320. (Photo by Brian Hodgson)*

providing students with the opportunity to experience transonic and occasionally supersonic flight, although this is more normally carried out when pilots convert to a front-line operational aircraft such as the Tornado or Typhoon.

The 'life expectancy' or fatigue life of a Hawk T1 is measured in flying hours. As built, each airframe is designed for a total of 6,000 hours. Through life-extension programmes, particularly in respect of replacing the centre and rear fuselage sections, the MoD authorized, in 1998, the funding to enable eighty airframes to have these hours increased, thereby enabling them to remain in service until 2012, the original out-of-service date (and the date that prompted this visual tribute to the type). At present the revised and extended out-of-service date for the Hawk T1 has been set at 2020. However, it will come

as no surprise to hear in a year or two's time that, like so many other decisions affecting aircraft in service in the UK, this will be brought forward, particularly as the RAF will not need as many fast-jet pilots.

* * *

Whilst there are a surprising number of discrepancies between published data (printed and online, including from the manufacturer) in respect of the specifications of the Hawk T1, particularly in respect of principal dimensions, what has been attempted below, but cannot be 100 per cent verified, is as accurate a specification for a Hawk T1A as possible. It is based primarily on data published in *World Air Power Journal, Volume 22, Autumn/ Fall 1995*. The principal technical specifications of the Hawk T1A in RAF and RN service are:

Crew:	1 or 2 (dual control)
Overall length:	11.85m (38ft 11in)
Wing span:	9.39m (30ft 10in)
Height:	4.0m (13ft 1in)
Wing area:	16.69 sq m (180 sq ft)
Wing track:	3.47m (11ft 5in)
Wheel base:	4.5 m (14 ft 9 in)
Thickness/chord ratio (root):	10.9%
Thickness/chord ratio (tip):	9%
Leading edge sweep:	26°
Quarter chord sweep:	21.5°
Internal fuel:	1,360kg (3,000lbs); 1,705 litres (375 Imp gal); 450 US gal
External fuel:	up to 380 Imp gal (460 US gal)
Stressing limits with full fuel:	+8G, -4G
Stressing limit with 1,360 kg (3,000 lb) external stores, plus 60% internal fuel:	+8G, -4G
Trainer take-off mass:	5,035kg (11,100lbs)
Maximum take-off mass:	8,350kg (18,405lbs)
Powerplant:	One non-afterburning Rolls-Royce/Turboméca Adour Mk 151-01 turbofan, rated at 5,200lbs static thrust (23.13kN), also quoted as 5,340lbs static thrust(23.672kN); by-pass ratio 0.8, SFC 0.7lb/lb static/hour.
Service ceiling:	15,2430m (42,000ft)
Range (internal fuel only):	2,400km (1,300 nautical miles)
Endurance (internal fuel):	3.5 hours
Range (external fuel):	3,150km (1,700 nautical miles)
Endurance (external fuel):	5 hours
Max speed:	555 knots
Armament:	1 x 30 mm Aden cannon pack (now withdrawn from service) Up to 2,540kg (5,600lbs) of underwing stores for rockets, bombs and missiles (some sources state 3,100kg, or 6,800lbs). Inboard pylons for up to two AIM-9 AAM Sidewinder missiles.

There are, or were, numerous options for external stores, including weapons fits. Whilst all were, in theory, useable by RAF and RN Hawks, they rarely carried them. This flexibility was mainly used by British Aerospace to promote the aircraft for potential overseas customers during their intensive sales drives.

Taken over Tal-y-Llyn lake from Corris Corner, part of The Mach Loop, as it starts its turn to port into the valley towards the village of Corris itself, is Hawk T1W, XX231, from 208 (R) Squadron, RAF Valley. This photograph shows that the gloss black finish is indeed high visibility, but only to this extent in good weather and light. At other times, particularly in the mountains, Hawks can sometimes be difficult to spot until the last minute. This must be the same for aircraft flying above a low-flying Hawk. This fine shot was taken on 5 August 2009. *Nikon D300; 300mm, 1/500 sec at f/4.0, ISO 200. (Photo by Meirion Williams)*

Above: Close-up morning shot of the rear of Hawk T1A XX256 as it awaits its next sortie at RAF Lossiemouth on 4 October 2012. *Canon 40D; 38mm, 1/800 sec at f/8.0, ISO 250. (Photo by Michael Leek)*

Opposite Top: Mid-afternoon close-up of XX188, 208 (R) Squadron, at RAF Lossiemouth on 4 October 2012. As always, Hawks are probably the best kept aircraft in RAF service. Rarely does one see exhaust stains, grease marks and other dirt on a Hawk. *Canon 40D; 56mm, 1/250 sec at f/16, ISO 320. (Photo by Michael Leek)*

Opposite Bottom: XX256 at RAF Lossiemouth again, 4 October 2012, but a more extreme rear close-up photograph – and with less of the inevitable but frustrating background clutter typical of most military airfields. *Canon 40D; 33 mm, 1/800 sec at f/8.0, ISO 250. (Photo by Michael Leek)*

The Hawk T2

Like the Hawk T1 and T1A, the Hawk T2 (originally designated the Hawk Mk 128) is a fully aerobatic fast-jet trainer – although in the present-day, jargon-rich marketing language of the MoD/RAF, the T2 is not a training aircraft, but a weapons platform. The design of the T2 builds on the Royal Australian Air Force Hawk Mk 127 and the South African Hawk Mk 120 (as will be seen in the photos in this book, the T2 is also very similar to the Indian Air Force Hawks). In the now frequently used obscure language of the MoD, 'the Hawk T2 is used to train selected personnel to meet the Fast Jet Operational Conversion input standards in order to contribute to the timely and sustainable delivery of capability'.

The cockpit of the Hawk T2 has advanced digital technology comparable to that fitted to current and future generations of operational fast jets, such as the Typhoon and Lightning II. Indeed, cockpit displays and instrumentation can be configured to mirror these fast-jet fighters. In modern terminology these new cockpits are known colloquially as glass cockpits, compared to the analogue systems fitted in the original Hawk T1s. With the T2 the whole nature of advanced fast-jet training has moved significantly forward compared to the T1, enabling the RAF to complete a more in-depth level of training that was previously not possible. This means pilots complete their fast-jet training better prepared for front-line operational aircraft. This has obvious cost-saving benefits because training on operational types will always be far more expensive than on trainers.

Whilst the engine is the same, it has been significantly up-rated, giving increased thrust and power-to-weight ratio.

More visible physical differences between the T1 and T2 include the lengthened fuselage, particularly the nose, which houses advanced avionics. The wing shape is also significantly different, not the least because of the wing-tip attachments, making a total of seven wing attachment points. The fin is another distinctive design change from the T1 in that it has a housing, or casing, for a forward passive electronic counter-measures system, similar to that fitted on the fins of Tornado GR4 aircraft.

Overall, the T2 is a more angular shape compared to the gently sweeping curves of the T1. As previously mentioned, the T2 does look more fit-for-purpose from a military aircraft perspective.

At the time of writing, the order for twenty Hawk T2s had been confirmed, with an option for a further twenty-four, all at an estimated cost of £3.5 billion (which has since increased, though this does include an extensive and service-life maintenance

programme). However, it seems that the total fleet of Hawk T2s will not exceed twenty-eight. This is probably in keeping with the premature retirement of the Tornado GR4, a reduced Typhoon fleet and a significantly reduced total for the Lighting II. With a much smaller number of front-line aircraft there will be far fewer new pilots to train.

The first flight took place in July 2006 from BAE Systems' Warton airfield, with the type formally entering service with the RAF at RAF Valley in April 2009, the first RAF T2 being ZK014. Before the aircraft could be used to train students it is of course necessary to have qualified flying instructors (QFIs) for the type, so between acceptance in 2009 and the start of the first course in 2012 selected pilots were trained as QFIs, the first instructor course starting in August 2010. Concurrently with the training of the QFIs it was also necessary to carry out post-acceptance trials, a continuation of the flight trial conducted by the manufacturer, BAE Systems, with 1,000 flying hours in the T2 being achieved by October 2010. All of these procedures, and many more besides, are the norm for any new military aircraft.

The first, and most likely only RAF squadron to operate the T2 and will be IV (R) Squadron, operating from RAF Valley. This squadron was, until relatively recently, a Harrier squadron, but was disbanded when the Harrier fleet was prematurely and incomprehensibly withdrawn from service, and sold at a bargain price to the United States Marine Corps (USMC) for spares, even though the airframes were all airworthy and had had extensive up-grades to enable them to remain in operational service until at least 2016. However, I digress, but such are the strange ways in which the UK's armed forces are 'managed' by politicians and bureaucrats alike.

IV (R) Squadron hoisted its colours again after being reformed at RAF Valley in November 2011, and celebrated its 100th anniversary in 2012 (for which two aircraft had specially painted fins, as shown in this book). Coincidentally, 2012 also saw the squadron achieve the 5,000th flying hour operating the T2, in September of that year. The first commanding officer of the reformed squadron was Wing Commander Kevin Marsh RAF, a former Jaguar pilot, and who, by privilege of rank, was the pilot of T2 ZK024 that passed the 5,000th flying hour. He was succeeded by Wing Commander Dan Beard RAF, another former Jaguar pilot and Hawk QFI, who took over in 2013.

The squadron is now a central or key unit delivering Phase 4 fast-jet training for the RAF and RN's Military Flying Training System (UKMFTS). UKMFTS is an outsourcing by the MoD of all future UK military air crew training to a consortium of

With traces of vapour being pulled from the wings on a grey, damp and overcast 1 April 2008, an unidentified Hawk from RAF Valley makes a dramatic and impressive pass through Cad West, in mid-Wales. *Canon 40D; 300mm, 1/320 sec at f/6.3, ISO 320. (Photo by Michael Leek)*

Above: Up close and personal. The extreme foreshortening caused by telephoto lenses enables dramatic close-up shots to be taken. Here an unidentified Hawk is caught on finals into RAF Lossiemouth on 17 March 2010. *Canon 7D; 400mm, 1/1250 sec at f/8.0, ISO 320. (Photo by Michael Leek)*

Opposite Top: Clearly demonstrating the fundamental difference between a low-level photograph to one taken at an air show or airbase is this shot of Hawk T1 XX156 from 208 (R) Squadron as it makes a close pass through Bwlch Oerddrws, in mid-Wales, on a fine late morning on 19 March 2009. (This photograph was used on the dust jacket of the author's first military aviation book.) *Canon 40D; 300mm, 1/800 sec at f/6.3, ISO 320. (Photo by Michael Leek)*

Opposite Bottom: An unidentified Hawk from 208 (R) Squadron, RAF Valley, makes a fine topside portrait on a low-level sortie during a late winter's afternoon on 1 March 2010. *Canon 40D; 400mm, 1/800 sec at f/9.0, ISO 400. (Photo by Michael Leek)*

Lockheed Martin and Babcock, known as Ascent. This is a unique initiative. It remains to be seen, through the twenty-five years of the contract between the MoD and Ascent, how effective, efficient and successful this outsourcing will be.

The first four student pilots – three men and one woman (Flying Officer David Wild, Flight Lieutenant Victoria Lyle, Flight Lieutenant Steven Moore and Flying Officer Thomas Wallington, all from the RAF) – successfully completed Advanced Fast Jet Training Course 001 on the T2 at RAF Valley in June 2013. This new course on a new aircraft, of eleven months' duration, included up to 120 flying hours and a comparable number of hours in the dedicated T2 simulator. To give an indication of the intensity of training, the following quote from the official MoD/RAF press release of 13 June 2013 gives a flavour of what the students had to achieve;

> There is no final examination as such, but the last trip on the course involves evading airborne and surface-to-air threats at medium and low level. The students then have to fly a Paveway IV bomb attack against a designated target whilst trying to evade a low level airborne threat. They then have to lead their wingman home in a simulated emergency.

The four RAF and two RN students on the second course graduated in August 2013. The current target for the UK is to train between twenty-eight to thirty RAF students per year and between four to eight RN pilots. This is apparently possible with the twenty-eight T2 airframes currently in service, even though this could prove inadequate if the planned growth in the number of overseas students is realized, but at the time of writing no decisions have been published as

to how RAF Valley, and IV (R) Squadron in particular, will cope.

The first overseas deployment of IV (R) Squadron's Hawk T2s was when three aircraft, six pilots and fourteen support ground crew went to the Finnish Air Force's training centre at Kauhava on 28 September 2012. For two weeks they operated alongside Finnish Hawks and the contrast in colour schemes was noticeable, with the RAF Hawks in their gloss black, whilst the Finns were flying their red and white aircraft, in a style that, from a distance, almost made them look like Jet Provosts.

In RAF service the Hawk T2 is proving to be a worthy successor to the T1, even though by service life standards it is still early days and, as with any new aircraft, there will inevitably be teething problems.

* * *

Unfortunately, it has not been possible to obtain as full a technical specification for the T2 as it has been for the T1, so what follows is a summary of the principal technical data of the Hawk T2 in RAF service;

Crew:	1 or 2 (dual control)
Overall length:	12.43m (40ft 93/8in)
Wing span:	9.94m (30ft 10in)
Height:	3.98m (13ft 1in)
Service ceiling:	13,565m (44,504ft)
Range:	2,520km (1,565 miles)
Max speed:	1,028km/h (638mph)
Engine:	6,500lb static thrust Rolls-Royce/Turbomeca Adour Mk 951 turbofan.
Armament:	AIM-9L Sidewinder missile, plus other stores and/or weapons.

The Red Arrows often fly low level between venues and to or from their home base at RAF Scampton, in Lincolnshire, in order for the pilots to maintain currency in low-level flying. This is notified in advance by the issue of a NOTAM giving precise routings and timings, albeit subject to local weather conditions. They normally transit as two formations of Five Arrow or Five Arrow, and Four Arrow with a singleton as lookout. On this occasion the lead Five Arrow formation is about to enter the tight Bwlch Llyn Bach pass in The Mach Loop in Wales, late on a Friday afternoon, 10 July 2009.

Formation flying at low level requires highly developed skills. The pilots must also have complete confidence in the skill of the lead aircraft as the outer pilots are not looking where they are going, but are instead concentrating on staying in position relative to the lead aircraft, trusting the lead to leave enough clearance from the ground. *Canon 50D; 300mm, 1/640 sec at f/5.6, ISO 400. (Photo by Brian Hodgson)*

Above: Pulling up fast and early from the Bwlch Oerddrws is Hawk T1A XX350, from 19 (R) Squadron on 7 February 2008. *Canon 40D; 300mm, 1/800 sec at f/9.0, ISO 400. (Photo by Michael Leek)*

Opposite Top: Most years at the Royal International Air Tattoo (RIAT) at RAF Fairford there is often a unique photo opportunity as the Red Arrows often fly alongside an aircraft type they do not normally perform with. In 2006 it was the turn of RAF VC-10 C1K XV104, from 101 Squadron, RAF Brize Norton. The VC10 had been painted with a red tail and inscribed '40 years of RAF service 1966-2006' to mark its long career in the RAF. The VC10 has now been retired from RAF service. Taken on 16 July 2006. *Canon 20D; 28 mm, 1/800 sec at f/8, ISO 200. (Photo by Brian Hodgson)*

Opposite Bottom: In relation to the completion of this book, this is one of the author's most recent Hawk low-level photographs, taken in Glen Tilt, Perthshire, on 10 October 2013, and shows XX200 from 100 Squadron. *Canon 7D; 300mm, 1/640 sec at f/9, ISO 400. (Photo by Michael Leek)*

Chapter Three

In service: the United Kingdom

The RAF

The primary role of the Hawk T1, T1A and T2 in RAF service is as an advanced fast-jet training aircraft for future Tornado GR4, Typhoon and Lightning II pilots. To quote RAF Valley's website (April 2013), the 'Hawk is used to teach operational tactics, air-to-air and air-to-ground firing, air combat and low-level operating procedures'.

Another major role for the Hawk is for operational support flying and for the advanced fast-jet training required for WSOs who will eventually convert onto the Tornado GR4 (although, as previously mentioned, this specific training is in decline as the Tornado fleet is being substantially reduced through premature retirement).

Number 208 (R) Squadron at RAF Valley is the largest squadron in the RAF. It currently operates seventy-one Hawk T1 and T1As. Combined with IV (R) Squadron, also at Valley, flying the Hawk T2, the two squadrons make up 4 Flying Training School.

One of the largest operational squadrons in the RAF also happens to be a Hawk operator: 100 Squadron, based at RAF Leeming in North Yorkshire, with eighteen aircraft. This squadron is responsible for fulfilling a range of different roles in support of other squadrons and units across the UK's armed forces. In particular they provide and act as an aggressor force, flying against other Hawks, the Tornado GR4, the Typhoon and helicopter squadrons. In other words they 'play' at being the enemy, thereby enabling others to develop their air combat skills. Because of these front-line roles 100 Squadron is the only Hawk squadron that does not have the suffix (R) after its number. Interviewed by *Air Forces Monthly* in February 2013, the then commanding officer, Wing Commander Christian Gleave RAF, summed up the roles of the squadron as being 'attack, aggressor, major exercise, trials, close air support (CAS), and domestic training, but the squadron also include[s] engagement and influence, when we're flying external agencies'[sic].

Pilots with exceptional flying skills have been known to be transferred to 100 Squadron halfway through an operational tour with a front-line squadron. Whilst this might suggest a less glamorous job for the pilot concerned, it usually means there are more opportunities to actually fly. For, example, a Tornado GR4 pilot is only *entitled* to fly seventeen hours per month; the word entitled being significant as this *doesn't* mean he or she will actually fly seventeen hours. Also, the flying on 100 Squadron is far more varied.

Subsumed within the squadron was the Navigation Training Unit for WSOs who were selected to fly the Tornado GR4 (indeed, the *only* aircraft they could fly in an operational capacity). With the draw-down of the Tornado fleet, the last course was completed in July 2012 as there are sufficient reserves of WSOs to see the Tornado through to the end of its service life with the RAF. (RAF career options for WSOs are not much brighter than they were for former Harrier pilots – an extremely expensive waste of taxpayers' money considering the extremely high costs in training modern aircrew.)

When 100 Squadron moved from RAF Finningley to RAF Leeming in December 1994 they did not take their RAF ground crew with them. Instead, all service engineers at Leeming are civilian, under contract to Babcock Aerospace, who are themselves sub-contractors to BAE Systems.

As previously mentioned, the original out-of-service date for the Hawk T1 and subsequent disbandment of 208 (R) Squadron, was December 2012. Revised dates were then stated as 2017, with the latest being 2020. It is the author's considered opinion that the Hawk T1 will be part of RAF history by 2017 at the absolute latest.

* * *

As will be evident, the RAF has almost always, and annually since the introduction of the Hawk, taken one or two airframes and had them painted in a special scheme for the annual round of air shows. As far as is known these schemes are designed from within the RAF and are applied following formal approval (which also includes approval by the Camouflage Working Group to ensure any design applied is safe under most

This Hawk T1W, XX167, in the markings of 208 (R) Squadron, has dropped down from medium height to join The Mach Loop just before what is known as Cad East, opposite the Cadair Idris mountain. Yet again, soft autumnal sunlight in late October shows how serene Snowdonia National Park can be. There is no doubt that low-flying training in this part of Wales must be a delight for pilots. This was taken on 23 October 2007. *Canon 40D; 340mm, 1/640 sec at f/5.6, ISO 250. (Photo by Michael Leek)*

Above: Hawk T1A XX203 from 100 Squadron, RAF Leeming, on finals into RAF Lossiemouth on a bright mid-afternoon on 17 July 2013. *Canon 7D; 200mm, 1/800 sec at f/10, ISO 400. (Photo by Michael Leek)*

Opposite Top: Another Hawk in commemorative colours; this time Hawk T1, XX318, from 100 Squadron, wearing the camouflaged scheme used by Avro Lancaster bombers flown by the squadron during the Second World War. In this photo, taken at RAF Lossiemouth, the Hawk was taking part in the Combined Qualified Weapons Instructor exercise held currently with exercise JOINT WARRIOR on 10 October 2012. *Canon 7D; 168 mm, 1/800 sec at f/6.3, ISO 320. (Photo by Michael Leek)*

Opposite Bottom: This Hawk T1A, XX285, from 100 Squadron, was being prepared for a sortie as part of the Combined Qualified Weapons Instructor exercise that was being hosted by RAF Lossiemouth when it was photographed on 9 October 2012. For this particular exercise visiting Hawks from 100 Squadron were parked alongside the hardened aircraft shelters (HAS) of 617 Squadron Tornado GR4s. The aircrew are completing pre-flight checks, whilst the ground crew prepare to remove intake covers. *Canon 40D; 200 mm, 1/800 sec at f/8.0, ISO 400. (Photo by Michael Leek)*

flying conditions). Some of these schemes work, others do not, though the author recognizes that this is very subjective, even for someone such as myself who has a visual arts background.

It would seem that many of the schemes applied to Hawks over the years are designed by individuals with no design or visual training. In addition, many designs completely fail to take cognizance of the actual shape of the aircraft. Far too many include the appalling and too frequent use of Times New Roman as the standard typeface, when one is needed – and Times New Roman is known to be one of the least easy to read, besides which it lacks any aesthetic qualities when used for display purposes. Fortunately a sans serif face is used by the Red Arrows, although I suspect this particular design was produced by a professional, not an amateur (who might have had a 'flair' for design!).

Sometimes the design of the annual Hawk display aircraft is actually that of the pilot selected to be that year's solo display pilot. In 2010, for example, Flight Lieutenant Tom Saunders RAF, then twenty-nine years of age, submitted his Union flag design that was accepted and applied – albeit with the awful Times New Roman lettering on the fin and on the air intakes. The author met Flight Lieutenant Saunders at RAF Valley early in 2010 and, understandably, he was not only proud to have been selected as the 2010 Hawk display pilot, but also to have had his design accepted and applied. Whilst the design proved popular with enthusiasts, Flight Lieutenant Saunders, who joined the RAF in 2004, did not complete the 2010 display season, as he was grounded. This was following a number of excessive manoeuvres that were considered dangerous due to the risk of him blacking out and therefore losing control of the aircraft. Not surprisingly, this was widely reported in the media at the time. The scheme designed by Flight Lieutenant Saunders is shown in at least one photograph in this book.

The scheme adopted for the 2012 display Hawk was designed by Jo Gough, a graphic designer. Through her design she endeavoured to reflect the fact that 2012 was the year of the Queen's Diamond Jubilee and the London Olympics. She combined this with the promotion of the main charity that supports RAF personnel and their families, the Royal Air Force Benevolent Fund (RAFBF). It was also a design that covered the whole aircraft as, inevitably, in most air displays at air shows the aircraft shows its topside less than the underside.

Unfortunately for enthusiasts there was no display Hawk for the 2013 season, although at one point it was expected that a T2 was to be used. For the record, the last Hawk display pilots are listed below and most, if not all, have been captured on camera with at least one photograph of each reproduced in this book.

2006: Flight Lieutenant Martin Pert was only twenty-five when he was selected to be the 2006 Hawk display pilot, thought to be the youngest pilot to be selected for this important public role. He joined the RAF in 2000 and became a QFI with 1 (F) Squadron, on the Harrier GR9, flying the last sortie on the type before it was prematurely retired in 2010. Flight Lieutenant Pert eventually joined the Red Arrows, taking part in the London 2012 Olympic flypast.

2007: Flight Lieutenant Mike Child joined the RAF in 2001 and following his fast-jet training became a QFI at RAF Valley, with 208 (R) Squadron. He has completed tours on the Typhoon, following which he was selected to fly with the Red Arrows.

2008: Flight Lieutenant Dave Davies. He joined the RAF in 1998 and, after a tour on the Tornado F3 with 111 Squadron at RAF Leuchars, he became a QFI on Hawks at RAF Valley for three years. At the time of his selection as the 2008 Hawk display pilot, it was expected that this was to be the final year for a Hawk display. Fortunately, this proved to be unfounded. Unusually, Flight Lieutenant Davies went straight from being the Hawk display pilot to be selected for a three-year posting with the Red Arrows.

2009: Flight Lieutenant Matt Barker joined the RAF in 1999. Prior to being selected as the display pilot he had completed one operational tour on the Tornado GR4 at RAF Marham. Later he became a Hawk QFI, graduating in 2006.

2010: Flight Lieutenant Scott Griffith (he replaced Flight Lieutenant Tom Saunders) joined the RAF in 2002. Flight Lieutenant Griffith, a New Zealander, previously completed an operational tour on the Tornado F3 at RAF Leuchars, followed by a tour as a QFI, also on the Tornado F3.

2011: Flight Lieutenant Juliette Fleming joined the RAF in 1999. She was the first female Hawk display pilot, having previously been selected as a Hawk QFI, following her fast-jet training on the type. She has also completed at least one operational tour on the Tornado GR4 at RAF Marham, which included detachments to Afghanistan.

2012: Flight Lieutenant Philip Bird joined the RAF in 2002. He has the distinction of being the very last Hawk T1 display pilot. At the time of his selection

Such are the sudden changes in the weather in mountain locations that even mid-day in mid-December it's possible to get good shots of landlocked aircraft. In this case an unidentified Hawk from 208 (R) Squadron shows its clean lines and polished surfaces against the matt backdrop of the opposite hillside. The smooth lines of the Hawk are evident, with no sudden or severe edges to break the flow; the Hawker pedigree is obvious. This was taken at Bwlch Oerddrws in The Mach Loop on 12 December 2007. *Canon 40D; 300mm, 1/1000 sec at f/2.8, ISO 250 sec. (Photo by Michael Leek)*

Above: Midway through its display routine for the 26 July 2009 Lake Windermere air show, Hawk T1 XX307, from 208 (R) Squadron, RAF Valley, in its 2009 display markings, makes yet another pass for the spectators along the famous Cumbrian lake. The houses of Bowness-on-Windermere certainly add to the effect of the aircraft literally passing your front door.

The RAF display Hawk would adopt different display markings from the previous years. This ensures the colour scheme is always unique. Also, a second airframe is often painted in the same scheme to act as a standby aircraft should an aircraft become unserviceable. Incidentally this particular airframe was also the 2007 display Hawk. *Canon 30D; 400mm, 1/500 sec at f/7.1, ISO 200. (Photo by Graham Farish)*

Opposite Top: The Red Arrows are frequent performers at the Dartmouth Regatta, in south Devon. In this photograph, captured from the east side of the River Dart a Red Arrow Hawk T1, XX322, shows its paces over the river, streaming smoke and contrasting well against a shadow-filled backdrop of the river bank, not far from the estuary. This was taken on 31 August 2012. *Nikon D300; 300mm, 1/640 sec at f/2.8, ISO 250. (Photo by Jamie Smith)*

Opposite Bottom: Experimenting with extremely slow shutter speeds can pay dividends as this example of the 2008 display Hawk, XX325, taking off from Duxford on 18 May 2008, demonstrates, even though it was an overcast day. The pilot is Flt Lt Dave Davies. *Canon 40D; 300mm, 1/80 sec at f/20, ISO 320. (Photo by Michael Leek)*

as the 2013 Hawk display pilot Flight Lieutenant Bird was a Tactical Weapons Instructor with 208 (R) Squadron. He has also completed an operational tour on the Tornado F3 at RAF Leuchars.

* * *

In addition to the schemes applied for air shows, some Hawks are painted in a scheme that celebrates a particular anniversary, such as the two Hawks flying with 100 Squadron that are, as near as possible considering the very different aircraft shapes, in the colours worn by aircraft from the squadron during the Second World War.

In most cases Hawks carrying a special paint scheme rarely go low level until the end of the season. Only then is it possible to get topside photographs; hence so many images of these Hawks in autumn or winter light. The reason for this is to avoid the risk of a bird strike which could not only ground the aircraft, but also damage an expensive paint job. Whilst I have not been as fortunate as I would have liked in capturing aircraft in these special markings, either low level or elsewhere, I have tried to include a reasonable cross-section through the photographs taken by the contributors to this book.

Squadron colours are another subject again. Many aircraft, particularly front liners, wear squadron colours that are often meaningless because the aircraft are pooled for use by other squadrons. This even happens with Hawks. Two or three years after a disbandment aircraft can still be seen wearing the colours of a squadron that is no longer extant, particularly with the Tornado GR4 fleet. It also seems, by the state of some aircraft, particularly Tornado GR4s and increasingly by the Typhoons too, that pride at squadron level is not what it once was. Maybe this is a reflection of the recent defence cuts and resulting redundancies that must have so demoralized many serving in the armed services. What pride can you feel or promote when your job is at risk at the whim of a Whitehall bureaucrat fulfilling the orders and policies of often ill-informed and sometimes naive politicians?

But one point is clear and that is having a fleet of fast-jet trainers painted in high-gloss black means that at least these do look reasonably well kept, suggesting pride at squadron level, even if the scheme itself is less than friendly for photographers. Bring back the red and white schemes of earlier years, or better, the camouflaged scheme worn by Hawks when RAF Brawdy in South Wales was active.

The Royal Navy
The primary role of the Hawk in RN service is to provide airborne threat simulation attacks against RN and other NATO warships and auxiliaries. These simulations include all possible scenarios that might be encountered on an operational deployment where there might exist a threat from enemy aircraft or ships and their weapons systems.

Another key role of RN Hawks is to contribute to the training of fighter controllers (FCs), through the Royal Navy School of Fighter Control, whereby FCs are responsible for directing friendly aircraft that are operating in support of naval vessels. Furthermore, RN Hawks are also used to support the training of RN Observers in Airborne Early Warning (AEW) missions.

Interestingly, the majority of RN Hawk pilots are civilian, under contract to the RN by Serco, an international service company that provides significant support to all three of the UK's armed services. Obviously, whilst they are now civilians, the Serco pilots all have military aviation backgrounds. The extent of their collective flying experience is best summed up by the fact that, as at August 2013, they had over 52,000 flying hours, mainly on fast jets.

The Empire Test Pilots School (ETPS)
Known as the ASTRA Hawk – Advanced Stability Training and Research Aircraft Hawk – this is used for variable stability training, which can be altered in-flight by the instructor, enabling the student pilot to make a live, or real-time, evaluation of whatever target or objective is being worked towards. With fly-by-wire technology, this Hawk is unique. It has been significantly altered from those operated by the RAF, RN and elsewhere, so that a single airframe may be used to simulate a variety of different aircraft handling characteristics, or to simulate adverse flying conditions.

Hawk T1 and T1A; RAF Units, Stations and Squadrons
The following list covers all known operators of the Hawk in UK service. Dates are the periods during which the specified unit or squadron operated the Hawk. In RAF service there are now only two RAF stations from which Hawks operate permanently, RAF Valley and RAF Leeming, although for operational and training purposes Hawks are frequently, albeit temporarily, deployed to other stations.

The R in parentheses stands for 'Reserve'. It is customary in the RAF for training squadrons and OCUs to be classified as Reserve squadrons to differentiate them from front-line operational squadrons.

1. Tactical Weapons Unit (TWU), RAF Brawdy, Pembrokeshire, Wales.
   79 (R) Squadron.
   234 (R) Squadron.

From many photographs of low-flying Hawks in various mountain regions of the UK it might seem that the light conditions are frequently poor, but this is not always the case, although poor light outweighs good, particularly from a photography perspective. Here Hawk XX165, from 208 (R) Squadron, RAF Valley, has been caught in reasonably good light, mid-afternoon on 1 July 2009. This photograph sums up the concept of low-flying photography in that the aircraft 'must' be landlocked. This was taken at Bwlch Oerddrws in The Mach Loop. *Canon 40D; 300 mm, 1/500 sec at f/8.0, ISO 250. (Photo by Michael Leek)*

Above: On 15 May 2012, twelve Hawk T1s of 208 (R) Squadron taxi down towards runway 31 at RAF Valley. The photographer, having climbed a sand dune, uses a 1.4x converter to great effect to foreshorten the view and in this case is thankful the sun was behind a cloud as the shot would otherwise have been ruined by heat haze. Eleven of these aircraft would formate to make up the 'R' in an 'E II R' formation that would form the centrepiece of a flypast at Windsor Castle the following Saturday, but on this occasion it was to be a full practice at nearby RAF Mona. *Canon 7D; 300 mm + 1.4 converter, 1/640 sec at f/8, ISO 250. (Photo by Brian Hodgson)*

Opposite Top: 2012 marked the sixtieth anniversary of the accession to the throne of Her Majesty Queen Elizabeth II and on 19 May 2012 there was to be a significant flypast over the parade ground at Windsor Castle. The centre piece of the flypast was a formation showing the Queen's official monogram, E II R. This was made up of ten Hawk T2s from IV Squadron (R) for the 'E', six Hawk T1s from 100 Squadron, the RN, for the 'II' and eleven Hawk T1s from 208(R) Squadron for the 'R'. A full-scale practice flypast was to occur at RAF Mona on the Isle of Anglesey in North Wales, close to RAF Valley, on 15 May 2012. As can be seen from the photograph of the practice day, the formation needed to be tightened up as the Hawk T2s making up the 'E' are slightly out of formation. *Canon 7D; 115mm, 1/500 sec at f/5.6, ISO 100. (Photo by Brian Hodgson)*

Opposite Bottom: The practice flypast to commemorate the Diamond Jubilee of the accession to the throne of Her Majesty Queen Elizabeth II was centred on RAF Mona on the Isle of Anglesey, Wales, on 15 May 2012. At nearby RAF Valley, no fewer than thirty Hawk aircraft would be launched, including eleven Hawk T2s; ten to make up the 'E' in 'E II R' and one spare. Seen here is part of the queue to get airborne with T2s ZK024 'O', ZK026 'Q' and ZK010 'A' visible amidst the engine exhaust. The Hawks would move en masse from RAF Valley to RNAS Yeovilton on 17 May 2012, which was closer for the actual flypast at Windsor Castle, held on 19 May 2012. *Canon 7D; 300mm, 1/320 sec at f/5, ISO 160. (Photo by Brian Hodgson)*

These two squadrons, and those of 2 TWU, had an emergency war role in that the Hawks could be used in a secondary air defence capacity, in which case they would be armed with Sidewinder missiles. This was during the late 1970s and 1980s in particular (i.e. during the Cold War).

2. TWU, RAF Chivenor, Devon, England.
    63 (R) Squadron.
    151 (R) Squadron.

No. 4 Flying Training School (FTS), RAF Valley, Anglesey, Wales.
    74 (R) Squadron.
    208 (R) Squadron.
    234 (R) Squadron.

No. 6 FTS, RAF Finningley, South Yorkshire, England.

No. 7 FTS, RAF Chivenor, Devon, England.
    19 (R) Squadron.
    63 (R) Squadron.
    92 (R) Squadron.
    151 (R) Squadron.

19 (R) Squadron
    RAF Valley, Anglesey, Wales: September 1992-November 2011.

63 (R) Squadron
    RAF Chivenor, Devon, England: August 1980-September 1992.

74 (R) Squadron
    RAF Valley, Anglesey: October 1992-September 2000.

79 (R) Squadron
    RAF Brawdy, Pembrokeshire, Wales: January 1978-August 1992

92 (R) Squadron
    RAF Chivenor, Devon, England: September 1992-September 1994

100 (R) Squadron
    RAF Wyton, Cambridgeshire, England: 1982-1993
    RAF Finningley, South Yorkshire, England: 1993-1994
    RAF Leeming, North Yorkshire, England: December 1994-to-date (still operational October 2013).

151 (R) Squadron
    RAF Chivenor, Devon, England: September 1981-September 1992.

208 (R) Squadron
    RAF Valley, Anglesey, Wales: April 1994-to-date (still operational October 2013).

234 (R) Squadron
    RAF Brawdy, Pembrokeshire, Wales.
    RAF Valley, Anglesey, Wales: two stations combined from 1978-August 1992.

The Red Arrows
    RAF Scampton, Lincolnshire, England: August 1979-to-date (still operational October 2013).

MoD (Director-General Test and Evaluation), A&AEE Boscombe Down, Wiltshire, England.
    Entry date of Hawk T1s (x 3) is not known, as the aircraft were rotated numerous times between the Test and Evaluation unit and other organizations/units.

Defence Research Agency – Aerospace Division, A&AEE Boscombe Down, Wiltshire, England.
    1980 (unconfirmed)-March 1994.

Test and Evaluation Establishment (T&EE), T&EE Llanbedr, Gwynedd, north-west Wales.
    1980 (unconfirmed)-1995.

ETPS, MoD Boscombe Down, Wiltshire, England.
    ASTRA Hawk (x 1): June 1981-to-date (still operational October 2013).
    Hawk T1s (x 2): December 1981-to-date (still operational October 2013).

Institute of Aviation Medicine, A&AEE Boscombe Down, Wiltshire, England.
    Entry date of Hawk T1s (x 2) is not known-November 1994.

RAF Centre of Aviation Medicine, MoD Boscombe Down, Wiltshire, England.
    December 1998-to-date (still operational October 2013).

British Aerospace (now BAE Systems), Warton, Lancashire, England.
    For product development and demonstration purposes BAE Systems and its predecessors owns or has owned at least seven Hawks (T1s, T2, Mk 50, Mk 100, Mk 102 and a Mk 200): 1977-to date (though it has not been possible to confirm how many, and of which type, are still flying).

Besides being a classic example of a low-flying photograph, this also demonstrates the height that is sometimes required by the photographer to get into a good position in order to maximise the visual impact of a low-flying military aircraft. Here Hawk T1 XX217, from 208 (R) Squadron, makes a low run, at a height of between 250 and 300 feet (76 to 92 metres), through the Cadair Idris pass in The Mach Loop. The photo was taken on 23 October 2007. *Canon 40D; 400mm, 1/800 sec at f/5.6, ISO 200. (Photo by Michael Leek)*

Above: With a good covering of snow in the valleys, 19 (R) Squadron Hawk T1A, XX286, is seen heading for the Bwlch Oerddrws pass in the Machynlleth Loop (The Mach Loop) in Wales on 1 March 2004. *Canon 10D; 400mm, 1/500 sec at f/10, ISO 200. (Photo by Brian Hodgson)*

Opposite Top: An HDR-processed image of Hawk T1, XX220, from 208 (R) Squadron, climbing to height above The Mach Loop on 19 July 2007. HDR was deliberately used to accentuate and pull out the form and shape in the clouds and to provide a wider perspective of the setting in which the aircraft is flying. *Canon 350D; 179mm, 1/800 sec at f/20, ISO 400. (Photo by Michael Leek)*

Opposite Bottom: In 2004 three Hawks were painted up for the air show season. The scheme chosen included the usual Union Flag but also celebrated thirty years of the Hawk in RAF service. Here we see Hawk T1A XX261 in the A5 pass at Llyn Ogwen, in Wales, on 11 August 2004, returning to nearby RAF Valley where the aircraft is based. This aircraft, along with similarly painted XX219 and XX159, were air show regulars throughout the UK and Europe in 2004. It is believed the 2004 Hawk display pilot was the late Flt Lt Jon Egging, who was tragically killed in Bournemouth, in August 2011 when flying with the Red Arrows. *Canon 10D; 300 mm, 1/500 sec at f/4, ISO 200. (Photo by Brian Hodgson)*

Hawk T2: RAF Stations, Units and Squadrons
No. 4 Flying Training School (FTS), RAF Valley,
Anglesey, Wales.
     4 (R) Squadron.

4 (R) Squadron
     RAF Valley, Anglesey, Wales: November
     2001 to date (still operational October 2013).
     Formerly a British Aerospace Harrier GR7/9
     squadron until disbanded in March 2010. It
     reformed as the first Hawk T2 squadron in
     2011. It is currently – October 2013 – the only T2
     squadron.

Hawk T1A; RN Stations, Units and Squadrons
Royal Naval Air Station (RNAS) Culdrose, Cornwall
(HMS *Seahawk*).
736 Naval Air Squadron (NAS)

This NAS was disbanded in 1972. It was
recommissioned following the merger of Hawks
from Fleet Requirement and Direction Unit
(FRADU) at RNAS Yeovilton, Somerset, with
the mixed Seroc and military-manned Hawks
at RNAS Culdrose, in June 2013. Regardless of
the merger, at least two Hawks from 736 NAS
continue to be permanently based at RNAS
Yeovilton.

FRADU, RNAS Yeovilton (HMS *Heron*), Somerset:
April 1995-November 1995

FRADU, RNAS Culdrose, Cornwall (HMS *Seahawk*):
December 1995-June 2013

On the last day of June 2009 the author was on Cad West, just below the Cadair Idris mountain in Wales, when this Hawk T1 from 208 (R) Squadron came through. Nothing special about the aircraft or the location – within The Mach Loop – but the image is typical of Hawks from RAF Valley in their element, demonstrating their excellent suitability as the RAF's fast-jet trainer of the late-twentieth and early-twenty-first centuries. *Canon 40D; 300mm, 1/800 sec at f/9.0, ISO 320. (Photo by Michael Leek)*

Above: Whilst the RAF is the oldest independent air force in the world (it was formed from the Royal Naval Air Service and Royal Flying Corps), the Royal Navy has been operating aircraft longer than the RAF and the RN wasted no time painting up most of their Hawk T1s in this attractive scheme in 2009 to mark one hundred years of naval aviation. Operating out of RNAS Culdrose, RN Hawks are often seen low level and, even if they are not marked as navy aircraft, the distinctive navy shoulder rank on the pilot's flying suit usually gives it away that it's being flown by the RN. Here Hawk T1A XX301 is seen in the Machynlleth Loop on 25 May 2010, entering the Bwlch Llyn Bach pass. *Canon 7D; 300mm, 1/640 sec at f/4, ISO 200. (Photo by Brian Hodgson)*

Opposite Top: Exercise JOINT WARRIOR, October 2012, and the Royal Navy Hawks from RNAS Culdrose start arriving at RAF Lossiemouth. In this shot a RN Hawk is captured on finals as it approaches runway 23 on 9 October 2012. *Canon 40D; 300mm, 1/1000sec at f/9.0, ISO 400. (Photo by Michael Leek)*

Opposite Bottom: A Royal Navy Hawk T1, XX301, home-based at RNAS Culdrose, Cornwall, rotates from RNAS Yeovilton, Somerset, on the morning of 11 July 2011, for a FRADU exercise sortie. Royal Navy Lynx helicopters, of the type frequently carried on deployment by destroyers and frigates, can be seen on the ramp in the background. *Nikon D300; 300mm, 1/640 sec at f/7.1, ISO 200. (Photo by Jamie Smith)*

Chapter Four

In service: overseas

The first overseas customer for the Hawk was the Finnish Air Force. Following a rigorous selection and evaluation process that included engineers and other ground crew as well as the obvious aircrew, they ordered an initial fifty airframes in late-1977, the aircraft being designated the Hawk Mk 51 (the order was subsequently increased by a further seven in late-1990). The unit cost for the first fifty Finnish Hawks was £2.56 million at 1977 prices.

Finnish Hawks are welcome visitors to RAF Valley, following a visit by IV (R) Squadron to Finland in September 2012. A return visit by the Finns to Valley was made in September 2013, enabling both Brian Hodgson and Jamie Smith to capture them low level through the Welsh mountains. Unfortunately, though, as with so many other air forces, the majority, if not all, Finnish Hawks are now a uniform grey, whereas before they carried a three-tone camouflaged scheme

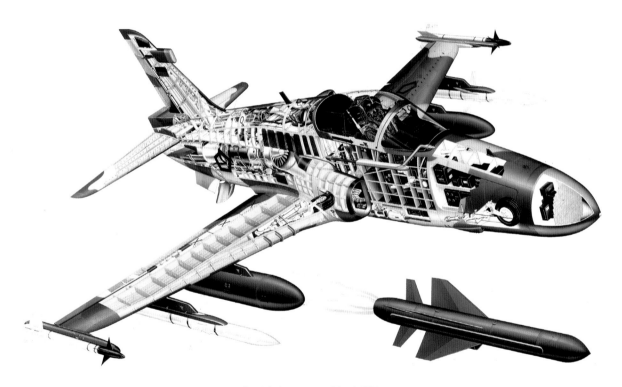

British Aerospace Hawk 200

This detailed full-colour cutaway illustration, drawn by hand, shows a Hawk 200 as designed and built by British Aerospace during the late-1980s. It is obvious that the design of this single-seat, lightweight, multi-role, low-cost aircraft has its foundations in the original two-seat Hawk T1, as widely used by the RAF and the RN. The most notable differences are the front fuselage, where the nose is larger – to accommodate a radar and enhanced avionics – and the pilot's raised position. Indeed, aft of the rear cockpit pressure bulkhead, the airframe is identical to a T1.

At the time the Hawk 200 was in production, only three air forces bought and operated the type. These were the Indonesian Air Force, the Malaysian Air Force and the Royal Air Force of Oman. The Royal Saudi Air Force was going to order but, it never progressed beyond the initial interest stage. British Aerospace expected sales to be higher, particularly from developing countries, but most of the air forces from these countries that were re-equipping wanted more advanced aircraft, even if they never really had, or have, a need for such complex technology (indeed, the situation is the same in 2013 with the new F-35 Lightning II, a stealth aircraft that most countries who've ordered it have no justifiable need to expend such vast sums of taxpayers' money on a still questionable aircraft – but everyone wants what they are led to believe is the best). (Illustration by Anthony S. Lawrence, Arts University Bournemouth, 1994, now: www.anthonys-studio.co.uk)

In beautiful winter light against a backdrop of a deep, dark blue-green forest, a Hawk T1 from 208 (R) Squadron, RAF Valley, approaches Bwlch Oerddrws in mid-Wales. Without the high-gloss finish that's applied to RAF and RN Hawks, shots such as this would not be possible. Furthermore, the gloss finish makes the aircraft visible, whereas if it was a matt finish the aircraft would be difficult to detect, be it from a hillside or from an aircraft above. Taken mid-morning on 25 November 2008. *Canon 40D; 300mm, 1/400 sec at f/8.0, ISO 320. (Photo by Michael Leek)*

A late-afternoon photograph of a Royal Navy Hawk T.1, XX244. This was taken from Cammoch Hill at 16:24 hrs on 28 October 2009, as the jet banked hard, heading for Loch Tummel. It was indeed fortunate that the sun had not quite set as there was still sufficient light to show off the magnificent autumnal colours of Perthshire. Canon 300D; 400mm, 1/1000 sec at f/5.6, ISO 800. (Photo by Iain Common)

Hawk T.1 XX318, from 100 Squadron based at RAF Leeming, is seen here on a cloudy, overcast morning. The aircraft was following the line of the A9, a few miles south of Pitlochry. This was taken on 27 August 2009 from a clearing in the forest that lies west of Pitlochry and Ballinluig. Canon 300D; 400mm, 1/800 sec at f/5.6, ISO 400. (Photo by Iain Common)

Hawk T.1 XX184 from 208 (R) Squadron, RAF Valley, making the most of the mountainous terrain on offer in Scotland as it banks hard and high heading west for Loch Tummel. The aircraft was photographed in perfect light from Cammoch Hill on 25 August 2010. Canon 450D; 400mm, 1/500 sec at f/14, ISO 400. (Photo by Iain Common)

A RN Hawk T1A, XX157, from RNAS Culdrose, in landing configuration as it comes into RAF Lossiemouth. This HDR image was taken during a JOINT WARRIOR exercise on 12 April 2012. Canon 7D; 200mm, 1/800 sec at f7.1, ISO 250. (Photo by Michael Leek)

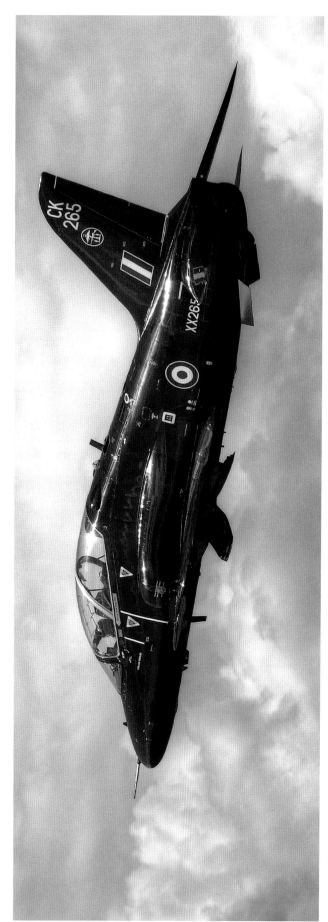

Another HDR image, but this time of a 100 Squadron Hawk T1A, XX265, taking off on 15 June 2008. Canon 40D; 200mm, 1/1250 sec at f/10, ISO 400. (Photo by Michael Leek)

Captured in beautiful and typically low winter late-afternoon light on 12 December 2007 is this unidentified Hawk T1, powering past The Exit, in The Mach Loop, Wales. *Canon 40D; 300mm, 1/1000 sec at f/4.5, ISO 320. (Photo by Michael Leek)*

The light might be poor and the air damp – and the photographer cold – but military aircraft low level amongst the rocks and heather make for impressive displays of finely-tuned flying skills. And here a Hawk T1, XX156, is put through its paces on yet another training sortie through the hills of mid-Wales. This was taken from the Cadir Idris pass, during late-afternoon on 1 April 2008. *Canon 40D: 300mm, 1/500 sec at f/5.6, ISO 320. (Photo by Michael Leek)*

An HDR image of a Red Arrow taking part in the team's display at the 2007 Royal International Air Tattoo (RIAT) held at RAF Fairford on 14 July 2007. *Canon 350D; 314mm, 1/1250 sec at f/10, ISO 200. (Photo by Michael Leek)*

On a damp, grey and misty afternoon on 13 September 2008, three Red Arrows roll down the runway at RAF Leuchars, led by Red One, as they depart to return to their home base at RAF Scampton, in Lincolnshire. *Canon 40D; 200mm, 1/160 sec at f/9.0, ISO 320. (Photo by Michael Leek)*

This is not an air-to-air shot, but shows, in the near perfect light of a summer afternoon, Hawk T1W XX313, from 19 (R) Squadron, level with the author who was located high above Bwlch Oerddrws in mid-Wales. This photo was taken on 21 July 2008. *Canon 40D; 300mm, 1/1250 sec at f/7.1, ISO 200. (Photo by Michael Leek)*

With the back-seater looking like he or she is enjoying the ride, Hawk T1W XX169 from 19 (R) Squadron, flies straight and level past Cad East, opposite the Cadir Idris mountain. Taken in summer light on 21 July 2008. *Canon 40D; 300mm, 1/1250 sec at f/5.6, ISO 200. (Photo by Michael Leek)*

Low-flying photography does provide better opportunities for taking images of an aircraft that can be composed in relation to the background, particularly if the aircraft is landlocked, as here. This is frequently not possible at air shows or when aircraft are grounded. In this shot, taken mid-afternoon on 23 October 2007, a Hawk from 208 (R) Squadron is captured approaching the Cadair Idris pass. *Canon 40D; 375mm, 1/800 sec at f/6.3, ISO 200. (Photo by Michael Leek)*

Also caught going through the Cadair Idris pass, but taken from the opposite side, known by the low-flying photography fraternity as Cad West, is Hawk T1 XX156, from 208 (R) Squadron. This was taken mid-afternoon on a dull 1 April 2008. *Canon 40D; 300mm, 1/500 sec at f/5.6, ISO 320. (Photo by Michael Leek)*

The Royal Saudi Air Force (RSAF) aerobatic team, flying Hawk Mk 65 and Mk 65A aircraft painted in a distinctive green and white scheme, was formed in June 1998 and is based at the King Abdulaziz Air Base (Dhahran). The team performed their first European display at Zeltweg, Austria, on 1 July 2011, where this photo was taken. This particular photo shows the team taxiing back to the ramp after completing their display routine. *Sony Alpha 700; 330mm, 1/640 sec at f/5.6, ISO 250 (Photo by Alexander Klingelhöller)*

In this photo, also taken at Zeltweg, three of the RSAF aerobatic team are about to rotate to perform their first European display. Compare with similarly composed photos of the Red Arrows elsewhere in this book. 1 July 2011. *Sony Alpha 700; 180mm, 1/320 sec at f/6.3, ISO 200. (Photo by Alexander Klingelhöller)*

Performing a low-level pass in less than perfect conditions during the 2008 display season is Hawk T1 XX325. This is one of the rare colour schemes that actually works, relative to the shape of the Hawk. In order to pull out shape and form in the clouds, this photograph has been converted to HDR. Taken on 1 May 2008, the pilot is Flt Lt Dave Davies. *Canon 40D; 300mm, 1/1250 sec at f/8.0, ISO 320. (Photo by Michael Leek)*

Keeping low whilst over-shooting the runway at RAF Lossiemouth enabled this portrait of Hawk T1A XX318, from 100 Squadron, RAF Leeming, to be taken on 25 August 2008. It has been converted to HDR. *Canon 40D; 400mm, 1/800 sec at f/10, ISO 400. (Photo by Michael Leek)*

Taxiing to 05, the short runway at RAF Lossiemouth, are two unidentified Hawks on a short-term deployment to Scotland. Behind are two Tornado GR4s from XV (R) Squadron, also waiting their turn to launch. This photo was taken on 22 February 2009. *Canon 7D; 400 mm, 1/400 sec at f/8.0, ISO 200. (Photo by Michael Leek)*

Against a backdrop of snow-covered hills, two Hawk T1As, XX313 and XX188, from 19 (R) Squadron, prepare to launch from RAF Lossiemouth on 17 March 2010. Behind the control tower can be seen the fins of three Tornado GR4s from the now disbanded 14 Squadron (although subsequently re-instated at RAF Waddington, flying Beechcraft Shadow R1s). *Canon 7D; 150mm, 1/800 sec at f/5.0, ISO 400. (Photo by Michael Leek)*

In dramatic summer light caused by the shadow of a passing cloud, this Indian Air Force Hawk Mk 132, still in its primer colours, goes through Bwlch Oerddrws on a test flight from BAE Systems Military Aircraft Division at Warton, Lancashire, on 18 July 2007. *Canon 350D; 200mm, 1/640 sec at f/8.0, ISO 200. (Photo by Michael Leek)*

Heading into the late-afternoon sun in October 2007 is Hawk T1 XX263, 208 (R) Squadron, on a solo sortie from RAF Valley. Taken from the top ledge on Cad East, opposite Cadair Idris, on 24 October 2007. *Canon 40D; 330mm, 1/800 sec at f/5.6, ISO 200. (Photo by Michael Leek)*

A three-ship take-off of Red Arrows in the colour scheme worn in 2007, when this was taken at a sunny RAF Fairford, Gloucestershire, on 14 July. The three Hawks are XX253, nearest the camera, XX292 in lead position, and XX266 on the starboard side. The quality of this formation take-off even extends to the undercarriages being retracted almost exactly at the same time. *Canon 350D; 140mm; 1/1000 sec at f/9.0, ISO 200. (Photo by Michael Leek)*

A rare line-up of four Hawk T1As from 100 Squadron, RAF Leeming, as they wait for clearance to launch from RAF Lossiemouth on 24 July 2013. From left to right the aircraft are XX258, XX203, XX346, with XX202 in the lead. Obviously they did not take off as one. *Canon 7D; 122mm, 1/500 sec at f/8.0, ISO 200. (Photo by Michael Leek)*

A clean, well-kept Royal Navy Hawk T1A, XX337, from RNAS Culdrose, Cornwall, clears RAF Lossiemouth for another JOINT WARRIOR sortie on 13 October 2011. The fin markings make it clear that the RN has a long track record of flying – probably the oldest military flying service in the world. *Canon 7D; 285mm; 1/640 sec at f/10, ISO 400. (Photo by Michael Leek)*

A line-up of four Royal Navy Hawks, from RNAS Culdrose, has been made ready for a lunchtime sortie from RAF Lossiemouth on 4 October 2012. As is evident in this photograph, Hawks, regardless of service, are probably the best kept aircraft in the UK's armed services inventory. *Canon 7D; 87mm; 1/1250 sec. at f/7.1, ISO 250. (Photo by Michael Leek)*

An unusual, or rare shot of eight of the nine Red Arrows in formation with three Supermarine Spitfires and a lone Hawker Hurricane. The four iconic Second World War aircraft are part of the RAF's Battle of Britain Memorial Flight (BBMF), based at RAF Coningsby in Lincolnshire. This HDR photo was taken on 14 July 2007. *Canon 350D: 154mm, 1/1250 sec at f/9.0, ISO 200. (Photo by Michael Leek)*

Hawk T1A XX246 from 100 Squadron, RAF Leeming, lines up on runway 23 alongside a Tornado GR4 from XV (R) Squadron for a late, grey afternoon launch on 1 April 2009. The aircraft did not take off at the same time, the Hawk going first. *Canon 40D: 107mm, 1/1000 sec at f/4.0, ISO 320. (Photo by Michael Leek)*

The world's foremost aerobatic team, the Red Arrows, taxi back to the ramp following a display in obviously less than perfect conditions – be it for general flying or for public display. As they do so, they are captured about to pass the last remaining airworthy Avro Vulcan B2 bomber, XH558, an iconic, historic and beautiful example of the aeronautical designer's 'art', and also the largest delta-winged aircraft ever to see active, front-line service. This was taken on 13 September 2009 at RAF Leuchars. *Canon 40D: 139mm, 1/500 sec at f/6.3, ISO 400. (Photo by Michael Leek)*

On a very wet morning on 17 March 2011 two Hawk T1As, from 100 Squadron, taxi for launching in an exercise held at RAF Leuchars (which will probably be closed by the time this book is published). In the foreground is XX198 and, about to turn onto the main runway, XX222. Enduring such weather conditions is essential if photographers want the unusual or the rare, particularly in Britain. *Canon 7D: 100mm, 1/500 sec at f/6.3, ISO 400. (Photo by Michael Leek)*

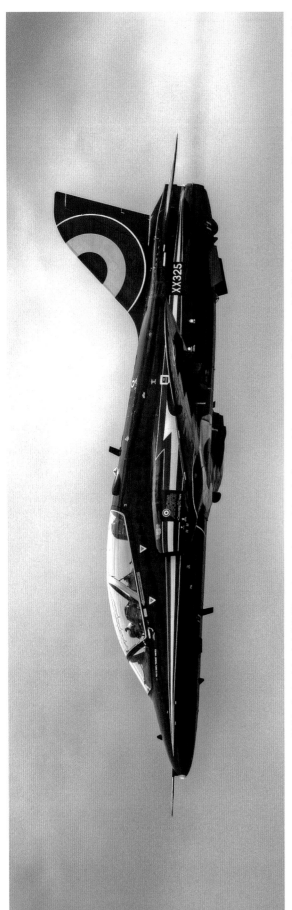

Making an impressive portrait is the 2008 display Hawk, XX325, as it runs fast and low in front of the camera at the former US Eighth Air Force base at Duxford, Cambridgeshire. This base is now one of the Imperial War Museum's out stations. This HDR image was taken on 18 May 2008. The pilot is Flt Lt Dave Davies. Canon 40D; 300mm, 1/1250 sec at f/8.0, ISO 320. (Photo by Michael Leek)

Another HDR image, but this time of a Royal Navy Hawk, XX281, on finals into RAF Lossiemouth, when it was taking part in a JOINT WARRIOR exercise on 18 April 2012. HDR was used to pull out the shape and form of the overcast sky, and some of the detail of what would otherwise have been almost a pure silhouette of the aircraft. Canon 7D; 200mm, 1/1000 sec at f/7.1, ISO 400. (Photo by Michael Leek)

Simplicity and naturally de-saturated colours often make for a dramatic composition. Here Hawk T1 XX181, from 208 (R) Squadron, RAF Valley, makes an imposing sight as it navigates towards the Cadair Idris pass in winter weather, on 11 February 2009. *Canon 40D; 300mm, 1/800 sec at f/8.0, ISO 500. (Photo by Michael Leek)*

A 19 (R) Squadron Hawk from RAF Valley climbs towards Bwlch Oerddrws on 17 December 2008. The bleakness of the landscape at this time of the year is symptomatic of what amateur photographers endure for the sake of their hobby. *Canon 40D; 300mm, 1/400 sec at f/9.0, ISO 500. (Photo by Michael Leek)*

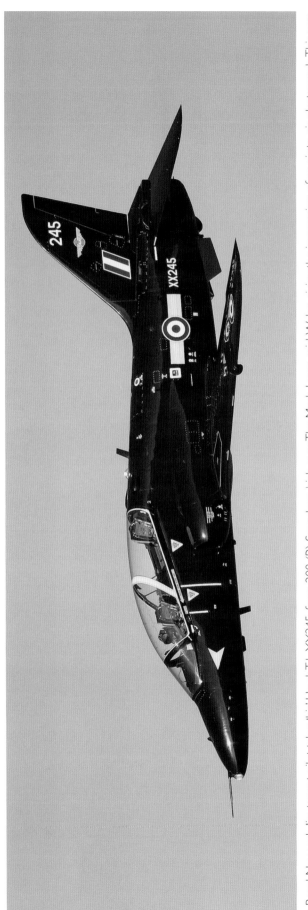

A Royal Navy sub-lieutenant pilot takes 'his' Hawk T1, XX245, from 208 (R) Squadron, high over The Mach Loop, mid-Wales, giving the impression of an air-to-air photograph. This was taken on 24 October 2007. *Canon 40D; 375mm, 1/1250 sec at f/6.3, ISO 250. (Photo by Michael Leek)*

At the point of rotating from the runway at RAF Leuchars on 13 September 2008, Red One, XX266, leads his team as they depart to head back to their home base at RAF Scampton, following a display in unavoidably appalling weather. *Canon 40D; 200mm, 1/160 sec at f/8.0, ISO 320. (Photo by Michael Leek)*

As previously mentioned, Hawks frequently fly in pairs as this is a necessary part of the training syllabus. Here two unidentified Hawk T1s from 208 (R) Squadron, RAF Valley, come through the shadows into late-morning sunshine on 8 May 2008 as they approach Bwlch Oerddrws in mid Wales. *Canon 40D; 300mm, 1/1250 sec at f/6.3, ISO 160. (Photo by Michael Leek)*

Hawk T1A XX174, from 208 (R) Squadron, makes a clean, straight and level pass through Bwlch Oerddrws on 12 December 2007. *Canon 40D; 300mm, 1/1000 sec at f/2.8, ISO 250. (Photo by Michael Leek)*

Profile shot of Hawk T1A XX307, from 208 (R) Squadron, in rare, bright sunshine, mid-afternoon on 4 March 2010. Even at this time of the year the snow from the winter can often linger long after it's disappeared from lower down where more sensible people walk. *Canon 40D; 250mm, 1/1000 sec at f/7.1, ISO 320. (Photo by Michael Leek)*

Heading south-west through the Cadair Idris pass, below Mynydd Ceiswyn, in The Mach Loop, this Hawk, XX195, 208 (R) Squadron, catches the mid-afternoon sun on 24 October, 2007. The white fleck is a sheep, who are never disturbed by the noise of low-flying military jets. *Canon 40D; 250mm, 1/800 sec at f/5.0, ISO 200. (Photo by Michael Leek)*

On a flat, grey day on 29 May 2008, Hawk T1W XX224, from 208 (R) Squadron, RAF Valley, pulls up to turn and eventually head north-east towards Bala in the Snowdonia National Park. *Canon 40D; 420mm, 1/1250 sec at f/5.0, ISO 400. (Photo by Michael Leek)*

Pulling up from Bwlch Oerddrws, XX313, 208 (R) Squadron, RAF Valley, turns towards the Cadair Idris pass as it navigates through The Mach Loop, mid-Wales. This was taken on 12 December 2007. *Canon 40D; 300mm, 1/1250 sec at f/3.5, ISO 200. (Photo by Michael Leek)*

that, with variations, was popular – and extremely effective in the landscape that prevails in Finland, and elsewhere in Scandinavia. Older Hawks in Finnish service also wore their original red and white scheme as recently as 2012, although it is not known if these have since been repainted.

Other countries soon followed, resulting in the Hawk T1 and its variants being probably the most successful advanced fast-jet training aircraft in the world, a lasting tribute to the designers at Hawker Siddeley. By July 2012, nearly 1,000 Hawks had been sold, and, in keeping with its Hawker pedigree, this is only second to the international success of the acknowledged pilot's aeroplane, the Hawker Hunter.

In contrast to the familiar two-seat Hawk trainer that frequents the skies of the UK is the Hawk 200. This is a single-seat, low-cost, affordable fighter and ground-attack aircraft developed specifically for developing countries and for those that were sensible and pragmatic enough to acknowledge that complex, high-tech, aircraft were an unnecessary luxury. Whilst the two-seat Hawk can be used as a front-line aircraft, and is in service as such with some countries, the Hawk 200 is a more advanced version with improved avionics and can carry an increased weapons load. Whilst there are no photographs in this book of a Hawk 200, there is a full-colour cutaway illustration. This has been included because, not only does this illustration show the differences, it shows the commonality between the two-seat and single-seat airframes.

The aviation industry in the United States of America has a reputation for rigorously defending and protecting its position as the prime provider of all military aircraft used by the armed services of the USA. This has sometimes resulted in decisions being made by the US government and the Pentagon that are at variance with the needs of the respective armed services, particularly the USAF (the most recent example being the replacement for the KC-135 Stratotanker). However, occasionally common-sense prevails and the right airframe is chosen. This happened when the Hawk was selected by the United States Navy (USN) in 1981 and, following extensive testing and the resolution of a number of significant technical and handling problems, entered service in 1992. In USN service the Hawk is known as the T-45 Goshawk and was built by a joint consortium between British Aerospace and McDonnell-Douglas. A total of 300 were originally requested by the USN, but this was reduced on a number of occasions due to budget constraints, and production stands at 214.

There are two versions of the Goshawk, the first being for land use only, the T-45B, and the second, the T-45A, is completely carrier-capable. To meet the demands for carrier operations T-45A Goshawks have strengthened airframes, stronger undercarriages, and more powerful and responsive engines – absolutely necessary for missed carrier landings. All Goshawks incorporate USN specified avionics, with cockpits redesigned by McDonnell-Douglas.

Whilst there were numerous problems during the early development and acceptance stages of the Goshawk's career (which are outside the scope of this book), now that these have been resolved, the Goshawk has proven itself a reliable, effective trainer and popular with the USN.

All USN Goshawks are all painted in a distinctive, high visibility red and white scheme.

USN Goshawks are nearing the end of their operational life and the USN is looking for a replacement (known as the T-X trainer). It is likely that BAE Systems will be marketing hard to have a navalised version of the standard RAF Hawk T2 accepted by the USN (a requirement that could be for as many as 500 airframes). Besides the need for an arrestor hook, it is not known if a navalised T2 will need a strengthened fuselage as the Hawk T1 did when it was converted or adapted to training at sea to become the Goshawk.

With flight testing for the new F-35 Lightning II well advanced (October 2013), it is necessary for the RN to have a number of qualified pilots ready to deploy on the new RN aircraft carriers currently being completed at Rosyth dockyard in Scotland. Eventually, RAF pilots trained on the F-35 will also deploy with their RN colleagues, in much the same way that the former Joint Force Harrier was operated by pilots from both services.

To develop their skills, a select number of RN pilots are training and flying with the USN on one or more of their nuclear-powered aircraft carriers. To qualify as carrier-competent pilots, RN and RAF pilots undertake initial training on USN Goshawks, usually flying out of Naval Air Station (NAS) Key West in Florida. The first stage of carrier training is done 'dry', with arrested landings being done at the NAS, before completing a number of day and night landings and launches at sea, again in the USN Goshawks. After this the RN pilots convert onto F-18 Hornets. Naturally, some of these RN and RAF pilots will become QFIs on the F-35, ready to train new pilots when the type eventually enters service in the UK.

As all RN and RAF fast-jet pilots complete their fast-jet training at RAF Valley on the Hawk T1 or, increasingly, on the T2, these pilots will obviously be familiar with the flight characteristics of the Goshawk.

Single-seat Hawks have not achieved the overseas sales expected by British Aerospace/BAE Systems, even though, at the time British Aerospace made a

The 2007 season Hawk display aircraft, XX307, takes a pleasing photograph as it approaches Bwlch Oerddrws late afternoon on 13 December of the same year. The 2007 Hawk display pilot was Flt Lt Mike Child, although at this late time of the year it was not necessarily him at the controls. *Canon 40D; 300mm, 1/1000 sec at f/3.2, ISO 400. (Photo by Michael Leek)*

Above: In clean configuration, reflecting late-afternoon light on 25 November 2008, Hawk T1, XX250 from 19 (R) Squadron, RAF Valley, contrasts perfectly against the dead mountain grass of winter. *Canon 40D; 300mm, 1/500 sec at f/8.0, ISO 400. (Photo by Michael Leek)*

Opposite Top: This commemoratively painted Hawk T1A, XX318, has already made an appearance in this book, but here it is on a low-level sortie through The Mach Loop, on the lovely morning of 6 September 2012. The scheme is a near copy of that worn by Avro Lancaster bombers flown by 100 Squadron during the Second World War. *Nikon D300; 300mm, 1/500 sec at f/5.0, ISO 200. (Photo by Meirion Williams)*

Opposite Bottom: The RAF Centre of Aviation Medicine at RAF Henlow operates two Hawk T1 aircraft, which fly out of MoD Boscombe Down, an aircraft and equipment testing facility in Wiltshire. The Centre of Aviation Medicine was formed in 1998, following a merger of the School of Aviation Medicine at Farnborough and the Aviation Medicine Training Centre at RAF North Luffenham, which closed in 1998. In this photograph, taken on 16 September 2009, XX162 is shown passing through Bwlch Oerddrws in Wales. *Canon 40D; 400mm, 1/500 sec at f/6.3, ISO 640. (Photo by Michael Leek)*

public announcement at Farnborough in September 1984 about their 'affordable fighter', there were enough countries interested for development to continue. Up to 1994 development costs for the single-seat Mk 200 had exceeded £150 million. All development work has now stopped and no new single-seat airframes have been built for sometime. One of the reasons for the poor sales has been the inadequate thrust of the engine, which makes it impossible to sustain very high rates of turn, an essential requirement in modern aerial combat. Only the Royal Air Force of Oman, the Royal Malaysian Air Force and the Indonesian Air Force have acquired the type.

As Hawk T1s and T1As are reaching the end of their service life with the RAF and RN, so are many in service with other air forces. Indeed, it will be noticed from the list below that some Hawks have already been retired, with more scheduled by the end of 2013. Very few overseas operators of the Hawk, if any, took advantage of life-extension programmes offered by British Aerospace/BAE Systems, meaning that once the designed fatigue life of the airframe is reached nothing is left but to retire and scrap it.

Abu Dhabi Air Force
    Hawk Mk 63; 38 aircraft ordered.
    Flying Training School, Maqatra.

Canadian Forces (NFTC – NATO Flying Training in Canada).
    Hawk Mk 115 (CT-155); 22 ordered.
    Moose Jaw, Saskatchewan.

Dubai Air Wing
    Hawk Mk 61; 8 aircraft ordered.
    Combat Wing, Mindhat.

Royal Australian Air Force (RAAF)
    Hawk Mk 127; 33 ordered.
    79 Squadron, RAAF Base Pearce, Western Australia.

Royal Bahraini Air Force
    Hawk Mk 129; 6 ordered.
    1st Fighter Wing, Isa Air Base,

Finnish Air Force (Suomen Ilmavoimat)
    Hawk Mk 51; 50 ordered.
    Hawk Mk 51A; 7 ordered.
    Finnish Training Wing, Kauhava, Western Finland.

Indian Air Force
    Hawk Mk 132; 106 ordered.
    Training Command, Bangalore, State of Karnataka.

Indonesian Armed Forces (Tentara Nasional Indonesia-Angkatan Udara)
    Hawk Mk 53; 20 ordered (to be replaced).
    Skadron Udara 15, Iswahyudi Air Force Base.

    Hawk Mk 109; 8 ordered.
    Skadron Udara 1, Supadio Airport.

    Hawk Mk 209; 32 ordered.
    Skadron Udara 12, Sultan Qasim II International Airport.

Kenya Air Force
    Hawk Mk 52; 12 ordered (all believed to be grounded).

Kuwait Air Force (Al Quwwat al Jawwiya al Kuwaitiya)
    Hawk Mk 64; 12 ordered (10 currently in service).
    12th Training Squadron, Ali Al Salem Air Base.

Royal Malaysian Air Force (Tentara Udara Diraja Malaysia)
    Hawk Mk 108; 10 ordered.
    No. 3 Flying Training Centre, Butterworth.

Royal Malaysian Air Force (Tentara Udara Diraja Malaysia)
    Hawk Mk 208; 18 ordered.
    9 Jehat Skuadron, Kuantan.

Royal Air Force of Oman (Al Quwwat al Jawwiya al Oman)
    Hawk Mk 103; 4 ordered.
    6 Squadron, Masirah.

    Hawk Mk 203; 12 ordered.
    6 Squadron, Masirah.

Royal Saudi Air Force (Al Quwwat al Jawwiya as Sa'udiya)
    Hawk Mk 65 and 65A; 50 ordered.
    11 Squadron, Riyadh (it is believed this squadron has been disbanded).
    21 Squadron, Riyadh.
    37 Squadron, Dhahran/Al Kharj (now believed to be at Riyadh).
    88 Squadron, Riyadh.

South African Air Force
    Hawk Mk 120; 24 ordered.
    85 Combat flying School, Air Force Base Hoedspruit.

A dramatic shot of Hawk T1A XX185, from 208 (R) Squadron, as it goes through Bwlch Oerddrws, piloted by the late Flt Lt Adam Sanders RAF on 9 October 2008 (for more information see the caption to the Frontispiece photograph). On this particular day Flt Lt Saunders made two passes. This is from the first pass whilst the frontispiece is from the second pass. *Canon 40D; 300mm, 1/800 sec at f/5.6, ISO 400.* *(Photo by Michael Leek)*

Above: Piloted by Flt Lt Mike Child is Hawk T1 XX307, from RAF Valley, in its 2007 display scheme. Following his tour as the Hawk display pilot for 2007, Flt Lt Child went on to Typhoons at RAF Coningsby before being selected to join the Red Arrows aerobatic team in 2012. This photograph was taken at RAF Fairford following the Royal International Air Tattoo on 16 July 2007. *Canon 350D; 100mm, 1/1600 sec at f/5.6, ISO 400. (Photo by Michael Leek)*

Opposite Top: A dramatic close-up of a Royal Navy Hawk T1A, XX217, from RNAS Culdrose, pulling up early as it navigates through part of The Mach Loop, in mid-Wales. This was taken from Bluebell, a hill that lies to the west of the village of Dinas Mawddwy, on 28 March 2012. Note that the front-seat pilot, probably a student, is reading the standard UK low-flying chart. *Nikon D300; 300mm, 1/1250 sec at f/5, ISO 250. (Photo by Jamie Smith)*

Opposite Bottom: Another photograph of the 2007 season Hawk display aircraft, XX307, taking a high pass through Bwlch Oerddrws, taken on 13 December, 2007. *Canon 40D; 300mm, 1/1000 sec at f/3.5, ISO 400. (Photo by Michael Leek)*

Republic of Korea Air Force (Hankook Kong Goon)
Hawk Mk 67 (T-59); 20 ordered (it is believed that in 2013 all were retired).

Swiss Air Force (Kommando der Flieger und Fliegerabwehrtruppen)
Hawk Mk 66; 20 ordered.
Fliegerschule 1, Emmen.

United Arab Emirates Air Force and Air Defence
Hawk Mk 61; 9 ordered (withdrawn from service).
Hawk Mk 63A and Mk63C; 20 ordered (withdrawn from service).
Hawk Mk 102; 18 ordered (withdrawn from service).

United States Navy (USN)
T-45 Goshawk; 221 ordered.
Training Wing 1 (VT-7 Eagles, VT-19 Fighting Frogs), NAS Meridian, MS.
Training Wing 2 (VT-21 Red Hawks, VT-22 *King Eagles*, VT-23 Professionals), NAS Kingsville, TX.

Zimbabwe Air Force
Hawk Mk 60 and Mk 60A; 13 ordered.
2 Squadron, Gwelo.

Overseas aerobatic teams:
Finnish Air Force (Suomen Ilmavoimat)
Finnish Air Force Aerobatic Team, Kauhava Air Base, Western Finland
4 x Hawk Mk 51A.

Indian Air Force
Surya Kiran Aerobatic Team, Bidar Air Force Station, Kamataka.
Hawk Mk 132 (believed to be withdrawn from aerobatics).

Indonesian Air Force (Tentara Nasional Indonesia-Angkatan Udara)
The Jupiter Blue Aerobatic Display team.
3 x Hawk Mk 53 (following a fatal accident, the Hawks were withdrawn from aerobatics).

Royal Saudi Air Force
Royal Saudi Air Force Aerobatic Team, King Faisal Air Base.
6 x Saudi Hawk Mk 65A.

In lovely low morning light on 24 October 2007 an unidentified Hawk T1 from RAF Valley is captured making a dramatic approach to the Cadair Idris pass in the Snowdonia National Park, Wales. *Canon 40D; 400mm, 1/800 sec at f/6.3, ISO 400. (Photo by Michael Leek)*

Above: A spotlessly clean Royal Saudi Air Force Hawk, 8806, from their aerobatic team, taxis back to the ramp, following the team's first successful display in Europe, known as The Airpower, in 2011 and hosted at Zeltweg in Austria. This was taken on 1 July 2011. *Sony Alpha 700; 100mm, 1/640 sec at f/8.0, ISO 200. (Photo by Alexander Klingelhöller)*

Opposite Top: The Hawk T1As of 100 Squadron are seen regularly in the UK low-level system, often working with forward air controllers or as hostile aircraft to be detected by fighters on combat air patrol. In 2007 the squadron painted XX285 to mark ninety years of the formation of the squadron and, fortunately for aviation photographers, it managed to keep this scheme for several years afterwards. The aircraft is seen low level leaving The Mach Loop at Bwlch Oerddrws on 18 April 2007 on its way back to RAF Leeming after a lunch stop at RAF Valley. *Canon 30D; 300mm, 1/1000 sec at f/6.3 + 1.4 converter, ISO 200. (Photo by Brian Hodgson)*

Opposite Bottom: Taking a more leisurely straight and level flight path than normal along Thirlmere Reservoir, this Hawk T1, XX285, from 100 Squadron, RAF Leeming, passes beneath the Helvellyn summit in some beautiful afternoon sunlight on 8 May 2008. This aircraft is unique as it was the only airframe to have these special markings applied, commemorating ninety years of 100 Squadron operations. *Canon 30D; 310mm, 1/640 sec at f/8, ISO 200. (Photo by Graham Farish)*

Chapter Five

The Red Arrows

The pedigree of the RAF's Red Arrows aerobatic team – arguably the finest aerobatic team in the world – has a long history. This history stretches back to the 1920s when, for example, 25 Squadron put up a nine-plane formation at the RAF Pageant at Hendon – the former RAF station that is now the site of the Royal Air Force Museum. This pageant was in 1926, although the first public display of what we today call aerobatics was in fact in 1920, also over Hendon. The aircraft used by 25 Squadron were Gloster Grebes, chunky-looking biplanes with rotary engines.

However, formation flying – the basis of all aerobatic displays – was started by the Royal Flying Corps, and others, during the middle of the First World War, in the days prior to the founding of the RAF in April 1918. It became apparent that, to increase a pilot's chances of survival in a combat or training situation and, by implication, his confidence in himself and the machine he was flying, it was necessary to make formation flying a pre-requisite of all military pilot training during the age of the biplane. The confidence-building aspect naturally extended to the individual pilot's colleagues within the squadron, and vice versa. It was only later that the public displays of formation flying became accepted, eventually becoming the norm at increasingly popular air shows and the like.

Specific teams from within the RAF during these early years included five Sopwith Snipes from the Central Flying School in which the aircraft were looped, rolled and flown inverted, yet throughout each sequence the aircraft remained in tight formation. Two years later, in 1922, five of the highly successful Royal Aircraft Establishment SE5As were the first to perform a formation spin. Another first was in 1929 when smoke was used to emphasize more clearly a formation's route through the sky. It was performances such as these that led to the RAF being one of the first air forces, if not the first, to establish an international reputation for the aerobatic skills of its pilots.

The 1930s – sometimes referred to as the Golden Age of Flight – saw the RAF publically perform with a number of aerobatic flights from different training schools and front-line squadrons. When the Hawker Fury biplane entered service in 1931 it became apparent that here was a machine eminently suitable for aerobatics, with 43 Squadron taking the lead with a display team of three aircraft.

A novel method of demonstrating to the public the skill of the pilots was for some teams to take off, perform and then land whilst being physically attached to each other by cords. For example, in 1933 25 Squadron took off with nine Hawker Furies tied together. Once airborne they broke into three sets of tied flights, and landed without having broken any of the cords.

The last three biplane teams were formed in 1938 with a trio each from 17 and 151 Squadrons flying Gloster Gauntlets, and 87 Squadron in their Gloster Gladiators, because the introduction of the monoplane into RAF service in the second half of the 1930s resulted in changes in flying tactics. This removed the need for the teaching and application of aerobatics as an essential part of a pilot's training and eventual abilities in air combat, although formation flying continued to be an integral part of the curriculum, as it does to this day.

The Second World War (1939-1945), and for a few years beyond, saw a halt to public displays by the RAF, or indeed any other service, and it was not until 1947 that three de Havilland Vampires from the Odiham Fighter Wing resurrected the practice of public aerobatic displays. The following year, 1948, saw 54 Squadron put up six Vampires. They toured the USA and Canada to much enthusiastic acclaim during that year's display season. It was also 54 Squadron who were the first aerobatic team to trail smoke from jets as an integral part of their routine. This was at the 1950 Society of British Aircraft Constructors (SBAC), at Farnborough, in Hampshire, when they flew five Vampires.

The de Havilland Vampire was replaced by the Gloster Meteor on the display circuit from 1952. This more graceful looking aircraft captured the public's imagination through the performances led by six aircraft from 600 Squadron. It was whilst the Meteor was in service and performing aerobatics that

From the perspective of photographing low-flying military aircraft this could be considered another classic view of a Hawk going through The Mach Loop in mid-Wales. In this example, Hawk T1 XX245, from 208 (R) Squadron, RAF Valley, is piloted by a Royal Navy sub-lieutenant, probably expecting, at the time this was taken, to be assigned to a Harrier squadron, only to have his flying career cut short by the still questionable decision to sell the UK's Harrier fleet cheaply to the United States Marine Corps, who used them for spares. This was taken on 24 October 2010. *Canon 40D; 375 mm, 1/1250 sec at f/5.6, ISO 250. (Photo by Michael Leek)*

Above: Two Hawks, XX288 and XX199, soon after launching from RAF Lossiemouth for a sortie in the Highlands. Taken on 8 September 2011 from the earthworks around the now ruined Duffus Castle in Moray. *Canon 7D; 400mm, 1/100 sec at f/8.0, ISO 320. (Photo by Michael Leek)*

Opposite Top: About to touch down onto runway 05 at RAF Lossiemouth is Hawk T1A XX255, from 100 Squadron, RAF Leeming, on 19 July 2012. *Canon 7D; 200mm, 1/200 sec at f/11, ISO 200. (Photo by Michael Leek)*

Opposite Bottom: A front fuselage close-up of an unidentified Hawk from 100 Squadron on finals into RAF Lossiemouth. This is an HDR image, taken on 24 July 2013. *Canon 40D; 400mm, 1/1000 sec at f/10, ISO 320. (Photo by Michael Leek)*

the first RAF team were given an official title; the Meteorites, from the Central Flying School at RAF Little Rissington.

Next in line as an aircraft that quickly became popular at air shows was the classic pilot's aeroplane, the Hawker Hunter, one of the most, if not the most elegant of post-war jet aircraft. The Hunter was introduced into RAF service in 1954, with 43 Squadron, the Fighting Cocks, at RAF Leuchars, in Fife.

However, it was 111 Squadron – the famous Tremblers, or Treble-One – at RAF Wattisham, in Suffolk, who introduced dedicated colour schemes specifically for aerobatic displays. This was in 1956, a year after the squadron started operating the Hunter. The colour scheme was overall gloss black. As a result the team became known as the Black Arrows. (The author considers himself fortunate to have witnessed the Black Arrows performing at what was probably his first visit to an air show, at Biggin Hill. His 'love affair' with the Hunter probably started from that moment).

Prior to the overall black scheme being adopted, various other colour schemes were tried, including at least one Hunter painted overall in red – a precursor to the Red Arrows colour scheme, though the Hunter also had the initials 'RAF' in large white letters on its underside.

Number 111 Squadron hold the still unbeaten world record for the execution of a loop using an incredible twenty-two Hunters. This extraordinary feat was accomplished at the SBAC show at Farnborough in 1958. That same year the squadron introduced the 'bomb burst', with the aircraft breaking formation at the end of a loop, trailing smoke, and pulling out in different directions. This is a manoeuvre that continues in the programme of the Red Arrows and remains as popular now as it was when first performed in the 1950s.

The Black Arrows performed until 1960 when the squadron disbanded before re-forming on the then new English Electric Lightning. With this new aircraft the squadron were tasked to concentrate entirely on operational air-defence duties and all aerobatic displays ended.

There were other units and squadrons flying displays with the Hunter, and other aircraft, including continued displays with Meteors and Vampires. Another famous Hunter team was the Blue Diamonds from 92 Squadron (the original name chosen was The Falcons, but this was changed in 1961 to its more famous name). Ninety-two Squadron used up to sixteen blue-painted aircraft, though by 1962, just before the squadron disbanded, they had increased this to eighteen aircraft.

Following the Hunter into RAF front-line service, and eventually into aerobatics was the English Electric Lightning, that most iconic and unique of British post-war interceptors, and sadly the last completely indigenous military fast jet to be designed and built in the UK. Number 74 Squadron – the famous Flying Tigers – was the first Lightning squadron to join the aerobatic circuit. This was in 1962, a year after the squadron had reformed and re-equipped with the Lightning. The Flying Tigers were soon followed by the Firebirds, of 56 Squadron, at RAF Wattisham. The author remembers seeing both 74 Squadron and 56 Squadron Lightnings performing at Biggin Hill. In those days aerobatic displays were far more exhilarating if only because there were no restrictions about flying over spectators. To experience a twelve-ship of Lightnings flying low, fast and in tight formation, often arriving from *behind* the spectators, was truly unforgettable, particularly to a young boy.

However, the Lightning did not last long as an aerobatic performer because of costs and operational requirements (the Cold War was reaching its peak in terms of tensions between NATO countries and those of the Warsaw Pact). It was far too expensive using front-line, operational air defence aircraft for what was nothing more than a public relations exercise, albeit a very popular exercise as far as the public were concerned. With the disbandment of 56 Squadron's Firebirds in 1963, it was decided that all subsequent RAF aerobatic flying would be by training aircraft.

In 1962, re-equipped with the T Mk 4 version of the British Aircraft Corporation (BAC) Jet Provost, the Red Pelicans of the CFS became the primary and official RAF display team. The aircraft were repainted from the then usual training scheme of silver and orange to an overall dayglo red. However, the Jet Provost lacked the natural aesthetic appeal of the Hunter or Lightning, and its popularity with the public never matched the previous aircraft, although obviously the skills of the pilots were never in doubt, and rightly so.

The SBAC show at Farnborough in September 1964 saw the first use of the Hawker Siddeley (Folland) Gnat in the aerobatic role. These Gnats were from No. 4 Flying Training School, at RAF Valley, Anglesey. These aircraft were painted bright lemon-yellow, and the name given to this team was the Yellowjacks, from a radio call sign.

In visual terms the Gnat brought back to the skies what the public perception of what most swept-wing military aircraft should look like, particularly in an aerobatic display. The swept wings and tail, sleek and slim fuselage, all made for a much smoother appearance, the aircraft's design contributing

With a cottage forming part of the backdrop, Hawk T1W XX283 from 19 (R) Squadron is seen in the turn following the A487 road south towards Machynlleth in the Snowdonia National Park in Wales on 2 April 2009. The T1W variant of the Hawk is a half-way house between the T1 and T1A and can carry the AIM-9L Sidewinder missile, but does not have bomb-carrying capability. *Canon 40D; 300mm, 1/640 sec at f5, ISO 400. (Photo by Brian Hodgson)*

Above: Part of the fast-jet training undertaken by Hawk aircraft at RAF Valley involves tactical flying, not just at medium or high altitude but also at low level. A pair of aircraft will fly to protect each other. This can involve the wingman constantly moving to protect the leader, flying on opposite sides of a valley or even flying at different altitudes to each other; it just depends on what task is being undertaken. Here we see two Hawk T1W aircraft, XX181 and XX175, from 208 (R) Squadron-lining themselves up to enter the Bwlch Llyn Bach pass in The Mach Loop in Wales on 27 May 2010. *Canon 7D; 300mm, 1/800 sec at f/7.1, ISO 200. (Photo by Brian Hodgson)*

Opposite Top: Weather conditions are not always conducive to spending long hours on a mountain in the hope of capturing a military aircraft low level, but sometimes the discomfort – and cold – is worth it. Here Hawk T1A XX286, 19 (R) Squadron, is photographed from Cammoch Hill in Perthshire, against the snow-covered hills around Killiecrankie towards Ben Vrackie on 18 February 2010. *Canon 7D; 400mm, 1/800 sec at f/11, ISO 250. (Photo by Michael Leek)*

Opposite Bottom: One of two Hawk T1s operated by the RAF Centre for Aviation Medicine is captured mid-afternoon on 24 February 2010 as it makes a dramatic run through a snow-covered Cadair Idris pass. These Hawks, based at MoD Boscombe Down, are frequent visitors to The Mach Loop in mid-Wales. *Canon 7D; 100mm, 1/800 sec at f/10, ISO 320. (Photo by Michael Leek)*

significantly to the visual impact of formation flying, whereas the Jet Provost, by its very design, never gave the impression of speed.

The handling qualities of the Gnat, and the fact that it proved to be very cost-effective, eventually led, in 1965, to the type being selected as the mount for a new RAF aerobatic team, the Red Arrows (whose official and formal title is the 'Royal Air Force Aerobatic Team'). The Red Arrows team was formed at RAF Fairford, Gloucestershire, with ten aircraft.

There is some question about the origins of the name Red Arrows, although the consensus is that red was chosen because, firstly, it was different to the lemon-yellow worn by the Yellowjacks (a name that was apparently not popular with some senior officers). Secondly, it was considered a colour of safety and it was also considered highly visible against a blue sky. The name 'arrow' was in recognition of the famous Black Arrows. Officially it seems the word red was in tribute to the Red Pelicans, although this has cannot be confirmed. Also, another reason cited for the new name was that red was the colour of the Flying Training School, under whose command the new team was to operate, whereas previously, aerobatic teams came under Fighter Command, partly because most aircraft were, up to that time, serving in front-line operational squadrons.

The first public performance of the Red Arrows was at Biggin Hill in May 1965 (witnessed by the author). The reception they received from the public was overwhelming and for the rest of that season's public flying displays the team received well-deserved praise. Indeed, by the end of 1965, the team had been awarded the Britannia Trophy from the Royal Aero Club in recognition of their displays and contribution to aviation.

What was to become a significant milestone in the Red Arrows' history was the appointment in 1966 of New Zealand-born Squadron Leader Ray Hanna RAF AFC (28 August 1928 - 1 December 2005) as team leader. Hanna went on to serve as team leader for three consecutive years and, after being recalled to take over again in 1969, became the only leader to serve four seasons, a record that stands to this day. He was awarded a Bar to his AFC for his outstanding leadership and airmanship.

Two years after his appointment, in 1968, Hanna increased the number of aircraft from seven to nine. This was to facilitate his determination to develop and expand the repertoire of display manoeuvres and sequences. The diamond nine formation was introduced during this time and has since become one of the team's trademarks.

The unequalled success of the Red Arrows under Hanna, and in his last year as leader, resulted in the Red Arrows being given the status of a full RAF squadron, but still under the auspices of the Central Flying School.

The team continued to operate the Gnat until the winter of 1979-80, when they took delivery of their first BAE Hawk T1s, but this was not until they had successfully performed 1,292 public displays in the Gnat, with their 1,000th performance taking place at the International Air Tattoo – now the Royal International Air Tattoo – at RAF Greenham Common, Berkshire, in 1977 (Greenham Common eventually ceased being an RAF station in 1993, primarily as a result of the end of the Cold War).

The Red Arrows team currently comprises ten pilots; Red 1, usually of squadron leader rank, a pilot who must have previously served with the team, through to Red 10. Red 1 is the team leader – or 'boss' – and Red 10, the 'road manager' (but also a qualified fast-jet pilot).

Competition to join the Red Arrows is fierce, with up to ten applicants for every vacancy, usually three per year. Understandably, however, the selection process is democratic, but extremely rigorous – and rightly so. It includes a final selection process – in camera – by the existing members of the team, a process that does not exist anywhere else in the RAF. The entry requirements include a minimum of 1,500 flying hours, at least one tour with an operational, front-line squadron (usually a minimum three-year tour of duty), and regular, above-average reports in terms of flying abilities and teamwork.

If successful, pilots can expect a tour with the team lasting up to three years and as there are three vacancies per year, the rotation sequence means there is always an overlap of six pilots in any one year, thereby ensuring continuity. This continuity is necessary to ensure that formation skills are maintained and for safety reasons.

In May 2009 the first female pilot was selected to join the team. This was Flight Lieutenant Kirsty Moore. Flight Lieutenant Moore joined the RAF in 1998 and following her fast-jet training on the Hawk T1 and a tour as a QFI, also on Hawks, both at RAF Valley, she was posted to XIII Squadron, RAF Marham, flying the Tornado GR4 (which included at least one tour on operations in Afghanistan). Whilst Flight Lieutenant Moore was not the first female to apply, she was the first to get through the necessarily tough but fair selection process, held at RAF Scampton.

Following the accidental deaths of two of her Red Arrow team mates, Flight Lieutenant Jon Egging and

Lunchtime on a lovely 29 May 2008 and Hawk T1W XX314, 208 (R) Squadron, goes through Bwlch Oerddrws. In good weather and conditions, as here, black-painted Hawks are clearly visible against the bright greens and purples of the surrounding hills. It's only when Hawks pass in front of pine forests that they can sometimes be difficult to track with a camera, particularly if there is little light reflecting off the aircraft's surfaces. *Canon 40D; 420mm, 1/1000 sec at f/6.3, ISO 400. (Photo by Michael Leek)*

Above: XX349, a Hawk T1W of 19 (R) Squadron, RAF Valley, is seen at an RAF Northolt photo shoot on 30 September 2010. This aircraft, along with several others, had been painted in 2010 to celebrate the ninety-fifth anniversary of the formation of the squadron in 1915. 19 Squadron was earmarked to receive the new Hawk T2s, but following the defence review of 2010, and the early retirement of the Harrier fleet, the Hawk T2s now carry the markings of 4 Squadron, which had been displaced from the Harrier. 19 Squadron disbanded in November 2011. *Canon 7D; 32mm, 8 secs at f/8.0, ISO 100. (Photo by Brian Hodgson)*

Opposite Top: An HDR image of an unidentified Hawk approaching runway 23 at RAF Lossiemouth. This aircraft was one of many taking part in exercise JOINT WARRIOR on 10 October 2012. JOINT WARRIOR is a major NATO exercise that currently takes place twice a year, primarily in northern England and Scotland. *Canon 40D; 30 mm, 1/800 sec at f/9.0, ISO 250. (Photo by Michael Leek)*

Opposite Bottom: Another HDR image, but this time of Hawk T1A, XX318 from 100 Squadron, RAF Leeming, as it comes into land at RAF Leuchars. This was taken on 17 March 2011 and converted to HDR in order to pull out the shape and form in the sky, and to add grain to the image. *Canon 7D; 220mm, 1/640 sec at f/11, ISO 400. (Photo by Michael Leek)*

Flight Lieutenant Sean Cunningham, in August and November 2011 respectively, Flight Lieutenant Moore voluntarily took on a ground role. Whether she has since returned to flying duties is not known.

In addition to the nine pilots, there is a support team of Team Manager, Road Manager (Red 10), a Public Relations Manager and Officer – who are both civilians – two engineering officers, an adjutant and about eighty-five engineering and supporting ground crew.

The engineering ground crew wear the now distinctive blue flying suits whilst the pilots wear the equally distinctive red suits. Prior to joining the Red Arrows, the ground crew will have followed normal RAF career routes in terms of specialist training. They do not join the RAF specifically to work with the Red Arrows. Of the ground crew, nine fly in the back seat during flights to and from display locations in order to carry out any necessary servicing prior to an actual display, and to service a pilot's flying gear. Each of the nine works alongside a specific pilot for the duration of that particular season's displays. They also fly in the back seats when the pilots are carrying out their required and vital low-level currency flights, as will be seen in some of the photographs reproduced in this book. At other times ground crew will fly a display sequence, again as evidenced in some of the photographs reproduced here. To be selected to fly in a back seat the ground crew must have demonstrated exceptional engineering skills and an above average commitment to the team.

When the Red Arrows perform outside the UK, be it in Europe or overseas, a number of the other ground crew and support staff will fly to the various locations in an RAF Hercules from RAF Brize Norton.

Reference has been made to the need for Red Arrow pilots to maintain their low-flying currency. This is because the majority will return to front-line squadrons on completion of their tour with the Arrows, and low-flying skills are a vital skill for all fast-jet pilots (and C-130 Hercules pilots too), particularly when a squadron is in theatre. Usually these low-flying sorties are undertaken at the end of the display season, in October or November, through the hills and mountains of Snowdonia in Wales.

Eleven Hawk T1A aircraft are normally allocated to the team; nine for displays and two in reserve, with one of the reserves usually flown by Red 10. The aircraft themselves are basically the same as those used by other RAF units and squadrons, with the exception of up-rated engines, providing pilots with a faster response time. The Arrows' Hawks also carry a smoke-generating system under the fuselage, in line with the main wing root. This smoke-generating system allows each aircraft to dispense five minutes of white smoke, one minute of red and one minute of blue. According to the official RAF website for the Red Arrows, the smoke is first and foremost for safety reasons, not for the benefit of the public. The smoke apparently allows the pilots to assess wind speed and direction, although it does raise the question as to why smoke trails were not widely used on other fast-jet aircraft used for aerobatic displays.

After forming at RAF Fairford in May 1965, the Arrows moved to RAF Kemble in 1966 and, subsequently, in March 1983, to RAF Scampton, Lincolnshire, where the squadron still resides.

The future of the UK's premier aerobatic display team is often the subject of debate, mainly, in recent years, because of the operating costs – £8.8 million sterling in 2009-10 (and probably an underestimate of the true costs). At 2011 operating costs this equates to approximately 259 flying hours for a Tornado GR4. Some have argued that the expense of the Red Arrows deprives front-line personnel of essential equipment, be they Royal Navy, Army or RAF.

A possibly more relevant argument might be that the running costs of the Red Arrows could be used to ensure a number of front-line aircrew would have sufficient flying hours to maintain not only their currency but also their safety. It has already been unofficially reported that the fatal Tornado F3 that crashed in Scotland in July 2009 was partly caused by the pilots of all F3s having their monthly flying hour entitlement reduced to twelve hours. The use of the word 'entitlement' means what is says; that it's not a guaranteed number of hours that will be flown, but merely what is authorized and budgeted for. This means that many pilots do not achieve their entitlement from one month to another. This was widely considered by aircrew to be not only insufficient, but also completely inadequate, particularly for safety reasons. Following the accident the government immediately, but belatedly, increased the monthly flying hour entitlement for F3 pilots to seventeen or seventeen-point-five, the 'norm' for a Tornado GR4 pilot, and probably for a Typhoon pilot too (although I've been unable to verify this).

The argument for disbanding the Arrows and using the resources elsewhere is that, as can be seen, the sheer cost of running a front-line fast jet is expensive, although £8.8 million doesn't go far.

The primary argument for retaining an undoubtedly expensive aerobatic team is the public relations benefits the Red Arrows bring to the UK and its industries, including the tourist industry. There is no doubt that, as the finest military aviation display team in the world, the Red Arrows do more for Britain

Pulling away from Bwlch Oerddrws and turning towards the Cadair Idris pass is Hawk T1 XX314, 208 (R) Squadron, on a bright morning on 29 May 2008. *Canon 40D; 420mm, 1/1600 sec at f/5.0, ISO 400. (Photo by Michael Leek)*

Above: It was generally regarded amongst aviation enthusiasts that the scheme chosen for the 2010 air show season was one of the best with its stylized Union flag design. Hawk T1A XX263 had barely got out of the paint shop when it attended one of the well-organized RAF Northolt night photo shoots on 25 March 2010. This was one of a pair painted in this scheme and a topside view of the scheme can be seen on sister aircraft XX201 elsewhere in this book. At the time this was taken the display pilot was Flight Lieutenant Tom Saunders, but he was eventually replaced by Flight Lieutenant Scott Griffith. *Canon 50D; 45mm, 20 secs at f/4.0, ISO 100. (Photo by Brian Hodgson)*

Opposite Top: Hawk Mk65A 8806, from the Royal Saudi Air Force display team, launches from Zeltweg, in Austria. This photo was taken on 1 July 2010 when the team made their first European visit. *Sony Alpha 700; 330mm, 1/500 sec at f/5.6, ISO 250. (Photo by Alexander Klingelhöller)*

Opposite Bottom: The Red Arrows have performed nearly 4,500 public displays since their inception in 1965, but in that time there have not been many opportunities to get images that are different from the normal air show view. However, on 24 July 2011 the air show at Windermere in the Lake District National Park presented such an opportunity. Here the Red Arrows are in Viggen formation, so called after the Swedish Viggen fighter, near the beginning of their display with the hills above Bowness-on-Windermere in the background. *Canon 7D; 300mm, 1/800 sec at f/6.3, ISO 250. (Photo by Brian Hodgson)*

than many other official organizations. Anyone who has witnessed the Red Arrows doing what they train for and what they are good at, even if they have no interest in aircraft, cannot but be moved by the sheer skill and professionalism of the pilots – and the ground crew who maintain the aircraft. One has only to watch aerobatic teams from around the world to recognize, even to the untrained eye, that the skill of the Red Arrows is second-to-none. This is particularly evident in the team's ability to hold position, regardless of the collective manoeuvre being flown at the time. Other aerobatic teams have a noticeable tendency to loosen up, almost to the point of breaking formation. This must be a confidence issue, for both individual pilots and for the team as a whole.

For the immediate future the Red Arrows are secure, for as recently as February 2013 the UK Prime Minister, David Cameron, stated on a tour of India promoting the Hawk aircraft, amongst other products, that he would guarantee the costs of maintaining the Red Arrows (at the time estimated to be in excess of £9 million per annum).

It was announced by the MoD, in June 2012, that the Red Arrows would remain at RAF Scampton until at least the end of the decade (2020). Whether the team continue to use the Hawk T1 or whether they'll be upgraded to the new Hawk T2 remains to be seen.

* * *

To conclude this introduction to the Red Arrows and their pedigree I would like to quote from the official MoD/RAF Red Arrows website (www.raf.mod.uk/reds/faqs/.cfm October 2013). It is from the section that explains the purpose of the Red Arrows:

> The Red Arrows are the public face of the Royal Air Force and are acknowledged as one of the world's premier aerobatic teams. Within the UK, the Red Arrows exist to demonstrate the professional excellence of the Royal Air Force and promote recruitment to the Royal Air Force. The Red Arrows have inspired a significant number of people to join the Royal Air Force, both as officers and airmen in all trades, not just pilots! The Red Arrows also help more than 500 UK charities every year – contributing many thousands of pounds to a wide variety of important causes.

Unless a pilot is aware or willing to provide topside photo opportunities at air shows, the norm tends to be boring bottom-side shots. Here, however, the pilot deliberately, or otherwise, presents the topside of Hawk T1 XX245 from 208 (R) Squadron, RAF Valley, as it banks sharply during a display at Kemble airfield in Gloucestershire. This HDR image was taken on 15 June 2008. *Canon 40D; 280mm, 1/1250 sec at f/5.0, ISO 200. (Photo by Michael Leek)*

Above: On a cold overcast day Hawk T1A XX247, 19 (R) Squadron, touches down at RAF Valley, in Anglesey, on 23 February 2010. There is nothing special about this photograph; it merely shows a Hawk returning from what it was designed to do – train fast-jet pilots. *Canon 7D; 100mm, 1/160 sec at f/7.1, ISO 160. (photo by Michael Leek)*

Opposite Top: A close-up of Hawk T1 XX181, 208 (R) Squadron, powering through the Cadair Idris pass on a winter's day; 11 February 2009. *Canon 40D; 300mm, 1/800 sec at f/5.0, ISO 500. (Photo by Michael Leek)*

Opposite Bottom: Quite literally popping out of the dark shadow of the Dinas Mawddwy valley within the network of valleys known to the aircrews as The Mach Loop, Hawk T1 XX307, from 208 (R) Squadron, RAF Valley, tries its best to show off its 2007 RAF Display Team markings in fading weak winter sunlight, as it routes towards the town of Dolgellau. Within less than thirty minutes this aircraft was already landing back at its base on Anglesey, a distance that would take at the very least two hours journey time by road, which highlights the speed the aircrews are travelling at. This was taken on 13 December 2007. *Canon 30D; 300mm, 1/800 sec at f/5.6, ISO 800. (Photo by Graham Farish)*

Chapter Six

Photographing the Hawk

Locations

The photographs in this book were taken at various locations in England, Scotland, Wales and a few in Germany. Specific dates will be found in the caption for each photograph.

The majority of the low-level photographs are from mid-Wales, including The Mach Loop, within what is known as LFA 7 (Low Flying Area 7). This covers the whole of Wales, in which TTA 7T (Tactical Training Area 7T) also lies. The Mach Loop itself lies close to the town of Machynlleth and is a flowed, anti-clockwise oval on which lie Cemmaes, Cwm-Llinau, Aberangell, Dinas Mawddwy, Bwlch Oerddrws, Corris and Machynlleth. It is flowed for safety reasons, although many years ago aircraft could enter at any point and in any direction, but following a number of fatal air-to-air collisions it was made one-way. Regardless of the fact that The Mach Loop is flowed – and clearly marked as such – some aircrew ignore the directions, running obvious risks. On more than one occasion the author has witnessed a number of RAF and USAF aircraft going in the wrong direction.

With the relatively close proximity of RAF Valley on the isle of Anglesey it is inevitable that The Mach Loop will have a large number of Hawk aircraft going through it, making it the best place in Britain to capture these aircraft on training sorties. Both types, the Hawk T1 and the new T2, are frequent 'visitors' to the area. There are several places from where many photographs in this book were taken, the most notable or widely used by amateur photographers being The Bwlch, or, more correctly, Bwlch Oerddrws, the highest pass in Wales and one of the narrowest choke-points, meaning that, with a 300mm lens, aircraft can fill the frame (although this is obviously dependant on the path taken by an aircraft). The Bwlch consists, more or less, of four ledges, each large enough to hold more than a few photographers and their kit. Moving on in an anti-clockwise direction the next location is known as The Exit, so-called because it is a point from which aircraft may continue following The Mach Loop or they could choose to exit by heading towards Barmouth and

the sea, via Dolgellau, turning north towards Bala, or simply climbing to altitude.

After The Exit the next two favoured locations are Cad East and Cad West, opposite each other and covering a narrow pass that is dominated to the west by the impressive Cadair Idris mountain. There are various vantage points on both Cad East and Cad West, but both can be problematic at different times of the day or year because of the position of the sun. Moving down in a south-westerly direction we arrive at a point where many aircraft turn to port, heading towards the village of Corris. At the point of turning, above the top end of Tal-y-Llyn lake is Corris Corner. Photographs taken from here often show the lake as a backdrop, evidenced in one or two photographs in this book, particularly by Meirion Williams. Between Corris Corner and all the way around to Aberangell, and south of Dinas Mawddwy, vantage points are limited because the valley is either too wide or the light would make it difficult; often it's a combination of the two, although the author has been successful above Aberangell.

Above the village of Dinas Mawddwy, both north and south, there are several suitable spots from which to capture Hawks low level, although to the author's knowledge the only person to frequent these is Graham Farish. However, light conditions and the fact that the view of approaching aircraft is comparatively restricted can create unwanted difficulties. Unfortunately, it was not possible to get a photograph of a Hawk to demonstrate the possibilities offered by these locations.

From Dinas, and before The Bwlch, is a ledge known to enthusiasts as Bluebell. This is a location favoured by Brian Hodgson and Jamie Smith, though not exclusively so. Both Brian and Jamie caught the Finnish hawks from Bluebell, when they paid a week's visit to RAF Valley in September 2013. The backdrop to photographs from here can be forest, farmland and/or farm buildings. Another reason why Bluebell is favoured is because most aircraft that enter The Mach Loop must invariably pass it, and usually at a height that's lower than the ledge itself, whereas all other

On a bright sunny day against a background of dead grass and the last of the winter's snow, Hawk T1 XX307, from 208 (R) Squadron, RAF Valley, shows off its distinctive shape to advantage. This was taken on 1 March 2010 from the top of Bwlch Oerddrws. It will not be long before the sight and sound of a Hawk T1 going through the valleys and glens of Britain will be history as this very successful fast-jet trainer reaches the end of its service life. *Canon 40D; 400mm, 1/800 sec at f/7.1, ISO 400. (Photo by Michael Leek)*

Above: In this shot Hawk T1W XX313, 19 (R) Squadron, does a touch-and-go, quickly gaining speed to launch into the circuit again. Taken on a grey afternoon, 23 February 2010. *Canon 7D; 80mm, 1/125 sec at f/10, ISO 160. (Photo by Michael Leek)*

Opposite Top: A bleak, cold late winter's day on 4 March 2010: the light almost gives the impression that this is a monochrome photograph. It shows Hawk T1W XX176, 19 (R) Squadron, pulling up frustratingly 'early' from Bwlch Oerddrws in The Mach Loop. *Canon 40D; 250mm, 1/500 sec at f/10, ISO 500. (Photo by Michael Leek)*

Opposite Bottom: In complete contrast to the previous photo is this unidentified head-on of a Hawk T1 as it powers out of the shadows and through Bwlch Oerddrws on 25 November 2008. *Canon 40D; 300mm, 1/400 sec at f/7.1, ISO 400. (Photo by Michael Leek)*

THE BRITISH AEROSPACE HAWK

locations run the risk that aircraft could leave early, climb high, or simply not drop down low enough to ensure a topside or landlocked photograph.

There are, of course, other areas in Wales from which it is possible to photograph Hawks. Where possible, these locations have been included in the captions. Graham Farish and Jamie Smith are particularly keen on researching and exploring new locations in Wales, usually by first observing a Hawk pulling out of an obscure or previously untried valley.

For ground shots, take-offs, approaches and landing photographs, Wales offers RAF Valley, on Anglesey, the largest RAF Hawk T1 and T2 station operating the types. Occasionally RAF Valley hosts enthusiasts' days where it is possible to get much closer to the action. Both the author and Meirion Williams have taken advantage of on-base opportunities to add to their visual record of Hawk aircraft. In addition, most of those contributing to this book have taken photographs from the perimeter fence, particularly from the north-western beach side, when the setting sun often provides added interest as it reflects on the high-gloss finish of Hawks coming in to land.

Photographs of Hawks taken low level in England are mainly from the Lake District, Cumbria, with one or two from the M6 pass, a few miles south of the village of Tebay. Some of these photographs are of Hawks on regular training sorties, whilst others were taken at the occasional air show that's held over Windermere. Another favoured low-level location within the Lake District is the southern approach to Thirlmere Reservoir, Dunmail Raise, and from various locations on the western side of the reservoir. As will be seen, there are numerous examples of Hawks photographed from these locations in this book.

Hawks regularly visit other RAF stations in England, for a variety of different training purposes. These stations might include RAF Cranwell, RAF Coningsby, RAF Marham or RAF Waddington. Also visited are RNAS Yeovilton, MoD Boscombe Down, and, amongst others, BAE Systems' airfield at Warton in Lancashire. And, of course, RAF Leeming, in North Yorkshire, is home to the Hawks of 100 Squadron and RNAS Culdrose is home to the RN Hawks of 736 Naval Air Squadron, reformed in September 2013. However, with the exception of photographs taken by the author, Brian Hodgson and Jamie Smith from or at RNAS Yeovilton, RAF Fairford, or at air shows in England, none of the aforementioned locations are represented in this book.

Air shows in England from where Hawks have been photographed include Kemble in Gloucestershire, Duxford in Cambridgeshire, Abingdon in Oxfordshire, and at RIAT, held at RAF Fairford, also in Gloucestershire.

Scotland presents a bigger challenge if only because the areas in which Hawks may fly low level is extensive, and the largest such training area in Britain. Because of this a stubborn determination is necessary, demonstrated primarily by Iain Common and Graham Farish, although the author too has captured Hawks low level in some of these areas, but not as extensively as Iain or Graham.

As mentioned elsewhere, Iain is a Scot and has spent his entire low-flying photography 'career' in Scotland, having a decided preference for particular locations in Perthshire and the Cairngorms. Graham, whilst from Yorkshire, has researched numerous obscure and remote locations in Scotland (and indeed throughout Britain), often with rare success, although obviously not always in respect of Hawk aircraft.

For photographs from the ground in Scotland, there is RAF Lossiemouth, in Moray, and RAF Leuchars, in Fife (to close in 2014, leaving RAF Lossiemouth as the last remaining RAF station in Scotland). Both host Hawks on a fairly frequent basis, with the former particularly so during exercises such as the bi-annual NATO Joint Warrior, held in April and October, although on an increasingly smaller scale as far as aircraft movements are concerned. Because the location of RAF Lossiemouth is close to the author's home, and is comparatively easy from which to take photographs, he has taken advantage of Hawk visits on a frequent basis. Furthermore, the station commander from 2011 to 2013, Group Captain Ian Gale RAF, was one of the few station commanders who, during his tenure, positively acknowledged the interests of military aviation enthusiasts by holding enthusiasts' days during JOINT WARRIOR exercises. These events, like those held at RAF Valley, provide rare opportunities to get close to the aircraft, and as JOINT WARRIOR involves both RAF and RN Hawks, it means getting close to aircraft from both services. Whether these enthusiast days continue under the leadership of Ian Gale's successor remains to be seen, but, with Typhoons replacing Tornado GR4s at RAF Lossiemouth from 2014, it is likely that the powers-that-be will restrict on-base access, in addition to restricting perimeter photography by the erection of higher security fencing.

Air shows are few and far between in Scotland, and those that are held are rarely attended by the author or contributors, so no photographs of Hawks from any of these locations are included. The exception is the annual show held at RAF Leuchars, but 2013 was the last of these long-standing shows. Whether RAF

Once an aircraft has navigated through Bwlch Oerddrws, in The Mach Loop, it suddenly and quickly comes out into a more open landscape. From here the options are turn right towards Bala, straight on over Dolgellau, or left through the Cadair Idris pass. This photo is of Hawk T1 XX303, 208 (R) Squadron, RAF Valley. It was taken on 30 May 2008. *Canon 40D; 420mm, 1/800 sec at f/7.1, ISO 640. (Photo by Michael Leek)*

Above: Taken from just below Brink Rigg, above Thirlmere reservoir in Cumbria, is this shot of Hawk T1W XX312, from 19 (R) Squadron, as it heads north on a cold morning on 9 April 2008. The author won't be climbing to this location again in winter, particularly because on this occasion the risk of snow became dangerous reality. *Canon 40D; 300 mm, 1/1000 sec at f/3.5, ISO 250. (Photo by Michael Leek)*

Opposite Top: Against a featureless sky, but catching the late-afternoon light on 10 October 2012, Hawk T1A XX189, from 100 Squadron, turns for finals on runway 05, RAF Lossiemouth. *Canon 40D; 300mm, 1/800 sec at f/9.0, ISO 400. (Photo by Michael Leek)*

Opposite Bottom: Dull, grey and sometimes dark days tend to predominate in the extremely variable weather conditions in the mountains when this photograph was taken, although the gloss finish helps separate the aircraft from its early autumn backdrop. It shows an unidentified Hawk T1 from 208 (R) Squadron going though Bwlch Oerddrws on 18 September 2009. *Canon 40D; 400mm, 1/640 sec at f/5.6, ISO 400. (Photo by Michael Leek)*

Lossiemouth will host an air show in the future is unlikely.

Outside of Britain, the only photographs of Hawks reproduced here are those by Alex Klingelhöller, from Germany. Alex's photographs are of the Royal Saudi Air Force's aerobatic team on the occasion of their first European tour. Whilst the display was excellent, typically for northern Europe the weather was less than ideal, but this is something we amateur photographers have to deal with on a frequent basis.

Of course, with the number of Hawks still employed by so many air forces around the world (see Chapter Four) there are, for the short term at least, opportunities to record these but, because of obvious geographical constraints, these are outside the scope of this book, besides which the focus or emphasis has always been on presenting a visual tribute to the Hawk T1 in service in Britain.

For more detailed descriptions of low-flying locations in Britain readers are referred to the author's book *Military Low Flying in the UK*, published by Pen & Sword in 2012.

Equipment

Each photographer has his or her own preferences, and no one can say for definite what is the best or most appropriate. So, what follows is merely the author's personal kit at the time of writing, based on advice from others, reviews and budget constraints. It is also worth noting that although the author's interest in military aviation photography was initially and exclusively through low flying, it soon extended to photographing aircraft at other locations, such as airfields and air shows. This has meant that, for both types of photography, a wider range of kit is necessary, particularly in lenses. Furthermore, comments are also based on the author's experiences with my chosen kit, and as such I recognize that some opinions will inevitably be subjective, but the point of this section is to provide a background to how the author's photographs were taken and with what equipment. As a visual tribute to a particular aircraft type, this book is as much about the aircraft – obviously – as it is about aviation photography, the means by which the visual element has been possible.

After an introductory period using a painfully slow Olympus 4-megapixel compact camera in 2004 and 2005, I followed this by the then more advanced Sony DSC-H5, which I bought with every known and available accessory. The Sony was purchased in 2006. The Sony served me well, particularly in getting used to the concept and nature of digital photography, not least having control over post-processing. Of note in terms of my digital introductory phase were

the satisfactory results achieved with the Sony on an extended trip at sea with the former Scottish Fisheries Protection Agency, a significant journey to Iceland, via Scotland, the Shetlands and the Faroes, and later a tour of north-west Scotland and its islands.

However, I quickly became aware that even the Sony was lacking in many respects. For aviation photography this was highlighted when I took this camera with me to RAF Lossiemouth. On the day in question not only were Tornado GR4s operating, but also the RAF Search and Rescue Sea King and a Chinook, the latter from RAF Odiham in Hampshire. Trying to capture sharp images of the helicopters yet still achieve rotor blur with the Sony was impossible. The combination was beyond the capabilities of the camera. The images were embarrassing.

Speed, greater control over settings, flexibility through interchangeable lenses and significantly higher resolutions were key factors in my deciding to move from even a flexible point-and-shoot camera such as the Sony, to a DSLR. In making this change I also decided on Canon, mainly because of what I perceived at the time to be a better range of lenses, not really having done sufficient research to establish that other manufacturers had an equally good range. My first DSLR body was a Canon EOS 350D.

With the Canon EOS 350D I also had the Canon kit lenses (rarely used because image quality from these lenses was very poor). Following research I had also bought the Sigma 70-200 mm f/2.8 EX DG macro HSM lens, which I still have and sill use frequently (in my experience this is a very good lens, though it has now been superseded by a mark II version). However, the limitations of the 350D quickly became apparent at the one and only air show that I attended with this body, even though, at the time, 2006, it was considered a very good DSLR for enthusiasts. Besides using this camera only once at an air show, I only ever used it on two occasions for low-flying photography, and some of the Hawk images taken with it are included in this book.

The 350D was followed by the Canon EOS 40D, almost as soon as it came onto the British market, and following an extremely positive review by the impartial website DPReview. Instead of getting the 40D with the kit lens, I opted for the Canon 17-85 mm f/4-5.6 IS USM lens, a very flexible lens that is ideal when you can get up close to the aircraft (although it has an apparent design fault in that the internal cable that enables autofocus to operate is prone to breaking after a number of shutter releases, but once repaired – but not by Canon – is usually good indefinitely). Soon after getting the 40D, I also invested in the Canon 100-400 mm f/4.5-5.6L IS USM. This was bought

A split background of a hill of dead grass and the dark forest green of the densely-planted pine trees provide the perfect matt backdrop to this Hawk T1W XX236, 19 (R) Squadron, captured in reflected light on 25 November 2008. This is a good example of how the gloss finish of the black-painted Hawks can be shown to advantage in a photograph. *Canon 40D; 300mm, 1/400 sec at f/11, ISO 400. (Photo by Michael Leek)*

Above: Hawk T1 XX198 from 100 Squadron levels out at the bottom of the valley towards Ullswater, having made the significant descent from the top of the Kirkstone Pass (a height difference of approximately 276 metres or 900 feet). The aircraft is carrying a modified 30mm Aden cannon (minus the cannon) under the centreline fuselage, which was not a particularly common sight on 100 Squadron Hawks. The Aden cannon has since been withdrawn from use. This photograph was taken on 1 September 2010. *Canon 50D; 400mm, 1/500 sec at f/7.1, ISO200. (Photo by Graham Farish)*

Opposite Top: Taken on 20 September 2012, this specially-painted Hawk, XX230, one of two so painted, is captured as it's about to touch down at Lechfeld, a Luftwaffe base in Bavaria south-west Germany. Both Hawks were specially invited guests at the Oktoberfest, an annual festival for friends of the base. The Hawk display pilot for 2012 was Flt Lt Philip Bird. *Sony Alpha 77; 210mm, 1/500 sec at f/8.0, ISO 100. (Photo by Alexander Klingelhöller)*

Opposite Bottom: On occasions aircraft fly higher or closer than the photographer expects, resulting in too great a focal length, particularly when using a fixed focal length lens. Here an unidentified Hawk in the markings of 208 (R) Squadron, piloted by a sub-lieutenant from the Royal Navy, goes straight and level through the Cadair Idris pass on 24 October 2007. *Canon 40D; 375mm, 1/1250 sec at f/5.6, ISO 250. (Photo by Michael Leek)*

specifically for low-flying photography, though in the low light that is almost synonymous with mountain locations in Britain, this lens is often far too slow, resulting in under-exposed photographs when using shutter priority. Nevertheless, this is a very good lens for use at airfields and air shows, where light conditions allow the lens to come into its own. Some examples are also prone to being soft, particularly when used at 300mm or above, although the author's example is fortunately sharp throughout the range.

Because of the shortcomings of the Canon 100-400mm lens, and by now being aware that for mid Wales and The Mach Loop in particular, a 300mm lens was considered the optimum, I invested in a Sigma 300 mm f/2.8 EX DG HSM . The Canon equivalent may be one of the finest lenses on the market but was far too expensive – and at 2013 prices is now definitely beyond my means. Whilst the optical quality of the Sigma lens might not be to the same standard as the Canon, it has served me well and continues to do so.

The quality of glass – the lens – is probably more important than the camera body, as long as the latter has at least 12 megapixels (and can shoot in RAW). The difference in image quality can be significant. Two contributors to this book now use the Canon 300mm f/2.8 lens, whilst another uses the Nikon equivalent. The Canon and Nikon lenses resolve far more detail than the Sigma equivalent, even on the same camera body. The differences will be apparent in some of the images in this book.

Nevertheless, with the Sigma 300mm f/2.8 lens, I also invested in the Sigma 1.4 x and 2.0 x convertors, the first of which is reasonably good, whereas the second struggles to give a semblance of a sharp image, even on a tripod and regardless of which Sigma lens I attach it to. Maybe I have just been unlucky. The point here is to test a lens or, in this case, a converter as soon as possible so that it can be replaced if not up to standard.

Other lenses acquired since the above include the Canon EF 400mm f/5.6 L USM, the Sigma 50mm f/1.4 EX HSM and the Sigma 10-20mm f/3.5 EX DC HSM.

Another significant investment was the purchase of another 40D and very soon after the Canon EOS 7D DSLR body. As with the first 40D the 7D was acquired as soon it became available in Britain. As with some of the lenses, the 7D was bought specifically for use in low-flying photography. Amongst a long list of options the 7D has an extremely fast shutter rate, a sensor of 18 megapixels, more accurate autofocusing and dual processors, making it an advanced semi-professional DSLR.

Additional equipment includes battery packs for each camera body, a monopod, two tripods (one standard telescopic and one 'miniature'), a BushHawk shoulder mount (useful in the hills), two dedicated camera backpacks, sensor cleaning kit, flash units and other items that the average but keen photographer of multiple subjects will acquire over a period of time.

Post-processing software, sequence and image quality

What follows has been written specifically in relation to how the images for this book were processed and made ready for print – as in converting from a processed digital image for printing in a book.

Some years ago, once I understood that there were very real image quality differences depending on which file format was used, be it in-camera or via post-processing software, I elected to shoot exclusively in RAW. Never again will I shoot in JPEG format – too much valuable and useful image data is lost because it is a compressed format that discards much that can be used or retrieved later (interestingly two of the contributors to this book still shoot in JPEG, whereas the others all shoot in RAW). Shooting exclusively in RAW means that every image will always require some form of post-processing via appropriate software. For the author this means Photoshop Elements, Photoshop CS4 or CS5 and Canon's own DPP (Digital Photo Professional). Much has been written about Photoshop, not the least that it is considered by many to be the 'industry-standard', although the introduction of what seems to be a very unpopular change by Adobe, whereby Photoshop users must now take out a monthly subscription to use the software, means many photographers are looking for cheaper and more flexible alternatives. There are undoubtedly many features in Photoshop that are very good, but it has to be acknowledged that Canon's DPP is also an excellent piece of software if it is used on the understanding that it's been designed specifically for digital photographs. Canon's software does not pretend to be for anything else.

For purely photographic image processing even Photoshop Elements has its place, regardless of what 'purists' might say.

The author's processing is carried out using two laptops and one desktop. These machines run the software, but for maximum visual control throughout post-processing, from organizing to final output settings, images are processed via a regularly colour-calibrated Dell Ultra Sharp U2413 monitor. This back-lit monitor is 60.96cm (24 inches) with a maximum resolution of 1,920 pixels wide x 1,200 pixels deep. It has been designed specifically for imaging editing and gaming.

* * *

Whilst this Hawk has, from the photographer's perspective, disappointingly pulled up 'early' from The Mach Loop, by sheer luck the top fuselage strobe navigation light has been captured, giving a natural focal point to this topside shot, even though the sky is almost and unfortunately featureless. It shows an HDR image of Hawk T1 XX217, from 208 (R) Squadron, RAF Valley on 17 October 2008. *Canon 40D; 300mm, 1/320 sec at f/13, ISO 400. (Photo by Michael Leek)*

Above: A detailed close-up of an unidentified Hawk T1 as it awaits clearance to launch from runway 05 at RAF Lossiemouth. Of particular note is the Aden 30 mm cannon in a centreline pod that also houses 150 rounds of ammunition. As previously mentioned, this pod has now been withdrawn from service. This photo was taken on 13 October 2011. *Canon 7D; 180mm, 1/400 sec at f/5.0, ISO 400. (Photo by Michael Leek)*

Opposite Top: In 2012, to mark the ninety-fifth anniversary of 100 Squadron, two Hawk aircraft were painted in a Second World War Lancaster-style camouflage scheme. 100 Squadron had three Lancaster bombers survive more than 100 missions, the most famous of these being EE139 'Phantom of the Ruhr'. The mission symbols below the cockpit on this Hawk were worn by 'Phantom of the Ruhr' and represent different mission types, red bombs being missions over Berlin, yellow other missions over Germany and ice cream cones being Italian missions. The skull and crossbones was adopted as the squadron emblem after the squadron returned from a French bar – or house of ill repute depending on your source – during the First World War, with a red flag portraying the skull and crossbones, although it wasn't officially recognized until March 1938. Here Hawk T1A XX318 was photographed leaving the Bwlch Oerddrws pass in The Mach Loop on 6 September 2012. *Canon 7D; 300mm, 1/800 sec at f/5.0, ISO 100. (Photo by Brian Hodgson)*

Opposite Bottom: Powering over Dinas Mawddwy on 11 March 2010, Hawk T1 XX245, in 208 (R) Squadron markings, is captured in the low setting sun, before disappearing back into the shadows of the valley.

One of the problems of photographing aircraft in the valleys if the sun is shining is the shadows created by the surrounding hills and mountains, particularly more so in winter when the lower angle of the sun is sometimes so low it cannot even penetrate into the deep valleys; the lack of light and trying to photograph a fast-moving object is not a good combination, due to the lower shutter speeds and higher ISO settings that will be needed to compensate to try and aim for a sharp image. *Canon 30D; 390mm, 1/500 sec at f/5.6, ISO200. (Photo by Graham Farish)*

After downloading images from the memory cards using Canon's Zoom Browser software, which automatically places each image in a date defined folder, images are rated according to sharpness, bearing in mind that all RAW files require sharpening.

The stages I use in the selection of images are loosely based on the following criteria:

1. Sharpness
2. Visual impact and composition
3. Setting (specifically those photographs in a low-level context)
4. Historical record (such as anniversary specials and/or commemorative schemes)
5. Information (showing the characteristics of the design of the Hawk)
6. Variety (linked to visual impact)
7. Resolution
8. Red Arrows.

The first has been dealt with above, whilst the second is clearly subjective as everyone has his or her own idea as to what constitutes a visually interesting or dramatic photograph.

The third criterion is more difficult to define because any military aircraft look better when landlocked in a low-level situation than anywhere else, except of course air-to-air photography, which is probably the best, but opportunities are effectively non-existent, except for the privileged few. Of course, the landlocked low-level aircraft scenario only applies to those aircraft that are actually operated in a low-level environment. Another factor in terms of this criterion is where the photograph was taken. If the aircraft does not fill the frame and there is a significant amount of the landscape visible then this has also influenced my choice. In this respect I have sought images for inclusion from locations in addition to the The Mach Loop.

Historical record, Information and Variety – criteria four, five and six respectively – are self-explanatory.

Resolution is extremely important. If a full-size, unedited image has less than 300 pixels per inch (or approximately 119 pixels per cm) across the width of an image in relation to the page layouts used in this book, then it has to be rejected regardless of how good the photograph is visually. This is because with anything less than 300 ppi detail could be lost. This was a particular problem on earlier DSLRs when the total megapixel count was lower than more recent models. It is also a problem when transparencies or photographic prints are scanned. In these cases a scan of 4,800 *dots* per inch is the minimum to retain maximum detail.

The final criterion combines all of the others with selections made on those images that demonstrate, where possible, what the Red Arrows are about, but avoiding too many of the type of photographs usually taken at air shows, of which numerous examples exist elsewhere.

In addition to the above, a small selection of photographs, all of them the author's, have been converted into HDR images (High Dynamic Range), using Photomatix Pro 4. Those images selected for this conversion were done for no other reason than that I considered the image would be enhanced by this additional post-processing because, as is now familiar to most, careful HDR manipulation brings out detail in both shadows and highlights.

Once selected, full-size images are adjusted, where necessary, in RAW mode, but always on a regularly colour-calibrated monitor (set at sRGB, with images converted to a recognized and compatible RGB profile, but never Adobe RGB). Adjustments might include exposure, light, tone, hue, contrast, etc., etc. The image is then finally sharpened, also whilst in RAW mode. This first stage sharpening is often referred to as capture sharpening. For most images I have my own preference settings.

The image is then opened and cropped to size. For this book this could be one of five different formats, for which I have determined the overall pixel width of each. The choice of format is determined, where possible, by the original composition or to create a more interesting or dramatic effect. To a lesser extent, another consideration might be space constraints within the book as a whole. In all cases cropping is done to actual reproduction size at 300 pixels per inch wide. The final part of post-processing is the output sharpening applied over a duplicate layer with a blending opacity of sixty-six per cent. Actual sharpening, using Unsharp Mask, is via my own presets. The image is then viewed at fifty per cent as this gives a more realistic idea of the printed image. What I look for here is evidence of halos appearing. If they are evident, then I reduce the amount of output sharpening.

However, for photographs taken in JPEG rather than RAW, in-camera sharpening may already have introduced halos and there's nothing that can be done to correct this – hence the need for photographers to always shoot in RAW.

Much has been and will, no doubt, continue to be written about sharpening. Part of the unresolved problem is that a digital image, composed of pixels, is not compatible with a printed image that's measured in dots per inch or lines per inch. The 617 Squadron Tornado GR4s that had specially painted fins to

From the looks of it, even fast-jet pilots can't be without their mobile phones, even on a low-level sortie! The back-seater in this shot looks very much like he's holding either a mobile phone or a compact camera, although I'm sure this is actually not the case. Text messaging can be addictive, but surely … The photographic conditions, whilst wintry, were almost perfect for a shot of a Hawk low level. Here XX256, from 19 (R) Squadron, heads west through The Mach Loop on 10 February 2009. *Canon 40D; 300mm, 1/800 sec at f/4.0, ISO 500. (Photo by Michael Leek)*

Above: On a brief deployment to RAF Lossiemouth on 31 July 2012 were a number of Hawk T2s in the markings of the recently reformed IV (R) Squadron, from RAF Valley. In this image a pristine Hawk T2, ZK020, is seen on finals as it approaches runway 23. This aircraft has been specially painted to commemorate the hundredth anniversary of IV Squadron. *Canon 7D; 168 mm, 1/1250 sec at f/7.1, ISO 250. (Photo by Michael Leek)*

Opposite Top: Here is the same aircraft as in the previous photo, but this time as it waits for clearance to join runway 05 for launching at RAF Lossiemouth. This photo was also taken on 31 July 2012. *Canon 7D; 70mm, 1/500 sec at f/7.1, ISO 200. (Photo by Michael Leek)*

Opposite Bottom: At the time this photo was taken, on 4 March 2010, this Hawk T2, ZK011, had not yet been handed over to the RAF but was still under the ownership of BAE Systems. It is shown here on a test flight through Bwlch Oerddrws in The Mach Loop. *Canon 40D; 200 mm, 1/1000 sec at f/5.0, ISO 320. (Photo by Michael Leek)*

commemorate the Dambusters' seventieth anniversary in 2013 were photographed for publicity purposes on a number of occasions. Most of these were air-to-air and were widely published. However, even though taken by a professional or semi-professional aviation photographer, there is still clear evidence of over-sharpening because clear halos on edges are visible. Indeed, there is no doubt that one or two images in this book might appear with halos, even though when viewed on a large monitor at the optimum size fifty per cent halos are not present, they might appear when the image is converted through the print process.

Personally, I believe we expect a level of sharpness in digital photography that is almost artificial. We certainly never expected the same from film-based photography, even from a studio shot. If you look closely at the internationally renowned photographs published in the US magazine *National Geographic* you will see that the images rarely have any trace of halos, but are comparable to quality film-based images. As for aircraft photography, one has only to look at the superb images taken by the late Charles E. Brown (1896-1982), one of the finest aviation photographers ever. A younger generation, brought up in the digital world, might argue that Brown's photographs are not sharp. I would suggest that his images are naturally sharp, because that's how the human eye sees the world.

Furthermore, the Internet is a very forgiving 'environment' on which to display photographs. A poor image in terms of exposure with slightly blurred edges can look almost excellent when even only minor adjustments are made through post-processing software, but the same image in print will look awful. Most images are displayed on the Internet at 72 ppi, whereas for a book or magazine you need an ideal minimum of 300 ppi. The difference between the two resolution settings is the reason.

Until the technology changes, the best way to judge the real quality of an image is through printing, be it through an ink-jet printer, or through a book or magazine.

This fine topside view of Hawk T2 ZK014, in IV Squadron (R) markings and coded 'E', sees it entering the tight Bwlch Llyn Bach pass (Cadair Idris) in The Mach Loop in Wales on 5 June 2013. Some differences between a T1 and a T2 can be seen here, the most obvious being the wingtip mounts to attach missile rails, the winglets on the rear fuselage and the longer nose. *Canon 7D; 300mm, 1/100 sec at f/5.6, ISO 160.* (*Photo by Brian Hodgson*)

Above: Detailed close-up of the front of Hawk T1 XX256 from 208 (R) Squadron as it sits in readiness for a lunchtime sortie at RAF Lossiemouth on 4 October 2012. *Canon 7D; 179mm, 1/640 sec at f/7.1, ISO 250. (Photo by Michael Leek)*

Opposite Top: A pleasing photo of Hawk T1A XX286, 19 (R) Squadron, as it climbs from Bwlch Oerddrws, piloted by the QFI in the back seat, whilst the student appears to be relating the aircraft's position vis-à-vis the low-flying chart for the area. Taken on 1 July 2009. *Canon 40D; 420mm, 1/640 sec at f/4.0, ISO 400. (Photo by Michael Leek)*

Opposite Bottom: On a dull, grey and damp 17 September 2009 Hawk T1W XX195, 208 (R) Squadron, on a solo sortie past what is known as The Spur. *Canon 40D; 420 mm, 1/800 at f/5.0, ISO 500. (Photo by Michael Leek)*

Photographer profiles

Iain Common

I have had a lifelong interest in military aviation. My father was a pilot in the Fleet Air Arm and Royal Air Force, ending his military flying career on the last Meteor NF14 Squadron at RAF Tengah. My earliest memories are of life on RAF stations in Germany and Singapore and, slightly less exotic perhaps, Kinloss.

I was very keen to follow in his footsteps but, discovering that I did not have the required aptitude to be a pilot, turned down the chance to join the RAF as a navigator (a decision I'm still unsure whether I regret or not).

The oil industry beckoned, however, and after spending fourteen years working in the North Sea I took voluntary redundancy in 1994 and have been working overseas since then, still in the oil industry but on a self-employed consultancy basis.

I have been taking photographs almost as long as I can remember. Visits to military airfields are now few and far between as I find it far more challenging and infinitely more satisfying to photograph aircraft at low level out in the wilds of Scotland. Now that the children have grown up and are pursuing lives of their own, the time off afforded by my present circumstances (and, more importantly, my wife's permission) allows me to combine a love of the outdoors with my passion for photography, spending many days perched on a windy hillside in Highland Perthshire waiting for that moment when a low-flying jet roars past (or lumbers in the case of a Hercules) at eye level or below.

I have an extensive library of military aviation photographs from as far back as the 1950s (Vampires and Meteors) right up to the present (Typhoons at low level).

Graham Farish

www.7001photography.com

Aviation, military in particular, has been a big part of my life from a very young age, having followed the interest my Granddad and his son (my uncle) had with aircraft.

They lived in East Anglia on the coast where there was a constant stream of military aircraft movements in the 1980s and 1990s, so it was impossible to ignore the over-flights even if you tried. Holidays at their home, would often be spent running outside into the back garden with a pair of binoculars and looking skyward to see what aircraft had just rumbled over their house.

The variation and the sheer volume of aircraft during those years was unbelievable, and as their location sat beneath one of the two main high-level exit and entry routes into and out of Europe, it was far from quiet in the skies both day and night. From four-ships of A-10s cruising over the top, F-111s skimming across the sea at very low level, to F-117 Stealth Fighters orbiting waiting for their tanker, to name a few. And not forgetting being woken up at 22:00 hrs one night by a pair of RAF Phantoms, dog fighting just off the coast. The full use of afterburner in the night sky made very impressive viewing despite me being ordered to 'get back to bed!'. Needless to say I never wanted to go back home from my holidays.

Returning home to West Yorkshire always felt like I would have an aviation drought once home, despite the fact that I lived in a low-level transit corridor where the weekday traffic consisted mainly of Tornado GR1s, along with varied other British aircraft to a lesser extent and, on occasions, even American A-10s. Most of the Tornado traffic originated from the TTTE (Tri-National Tornado Training Establishment) at RAF Cottesmore, where the RAF, German and Italian aircrews were trained to fly the Tornado.

Because of the need to train, there was plenty of Tornado flying taking place over my village from as early as 08:30 in the morning up until 23:00 if they were night flying, as the crews transited through at low level to the north of England and beyond. I took video camera footage of some of these overflights too.

My school was also within the transit corridor, so leaning back on my chair in lessons happened very often, just to get a glance out of the window at the aircraft that had just gone over. Inevitably, I nearly always got into trouble for not paying attention; however some teachers strangely understood my bad habit.

Using a slower than usual shutter speed creates a greater sense of speed as this unidentified Hawk T1W from 19 (R) Squadron powers past a location known by amateur low-flying photographers as The Exit, immediately following Bwlch Oerddrws, in The Mach Loop, mid-Wales. This was taken on a very dull day, 17 October 2008. *Canon 40D; 300mm, 1/250 sec at f/8.0, ISO 400. (Photo by Michael Leek)*

Above: Hawk T1W XX176, 19 (R) Squadron, carrying the centreline Aden 30mm cannon pod that has since been withdrawn from service, makes a fast, straight and level pass through Cad East. This aircraft also has CBLS-100 practice-bomb carriers on each wing. Taken on 17 December 2008. *Canon 40D; 300mm, 1/400 sec at f/5.0, ISO 500. (Photo by Michael Leek)*

Opposite Top: An atmospheric shot of an unidentified Hawk T1 as it pulls up from The Mach Loop because of poor visibility through the low-lying cloud. Taken at lunchtime on 17 December 2008. *Canon 40D; 300mm, 1/400 sec at f/6.3, ISO 500. (Photo by Michael Leek)*

Opposite Bottom: A less aggressive angle of attack through Cad West is demonstrated by Hawk T1 XX181, 208 (R) Squadron, on 11 February 2009. The white flecks on the hill behind are snow. *Canon 40D; 300mm, 1/800 sec at f/4.0, ISO 500. (Photo by Michael Leek)*

I even used to take an air-band radio to school so that I could sit outside and listen out for aircraft during break times.

I have good memories from those years, one in particular when a German Navy Tornado passed by at low level, which was relatively rare to see over the village. The grey/white markings were clearly visible which confirmed this, but also seeing the white helmets that the aircrew were wearing, with the naked eye, indicated that they were probably a little lower than they should have been. Seeing a Tornado approaching the house at low level completely on its side trailing smoke in silence, followed by the roar of engines, is something that will stick with me forever. This is probably one of the connections as to why I found an interest in low-flying photography, and for having a fondness for the Tornado.

In 1999 RAF Cottesmore ceased Tornado operations and the low-level route over my house sadly became much quieter.

Despite all this aviation activity and partly because I was too young to be able to drive a car to get out and about easily, I actually started aviation still photography much later with a very basic camera at air bases. I soon got very bored of landing and take-off shots and I realized that I needed to inject some more excitement into my day trips. So I decided to give photography in the valleys another go, having been unsuccessful with a video camera a few years previously. The offer of borrowing an SLR camera and lens from my Dad was all it took. The bug had bitten.

I then followed this up by buying my own camera equipment very shortly afterwards and there was no looking back. The air bases had lost what little appeal they had for me, with the mountains and valleys always being my primary place to go.

Not knowing if an aircraft will even show up in the valley that has been selected is one of the reasons that still drives my obsession to this day, particularly more so at a new and untried location, where there is probably less guarantee.

Having imagined what an aircraft's position should look like in the valley prior to trying a new location, along with hoping that the height climbed is sufficient and what camera settings and lens combination will be required, not forgetting the weather conditions for the day, plus the sun's position if it is shining, for me, all add to the unpredictability.

This could perhaps be seen as a form of self torture, but when everything does go as planned it can be extremely rewarding when the efforts and planning pay off.

My camera setup has always been Canon, using the 300D with a Tamron 100-400mm lens originally.

The Tamron was an OK lens but the autofocus often seemed sluggish and opportunities were missed, so I upgraded to a Canon 30D and the Canon 100-400mm L IS lens. This was a very good combination in good light, but during low light, which is common in the mountains, the max aperture of f/5.6 was restrictive, giving very slow shutter speeds. Adding a Bushhawk 'rifle type grip' to my setup and locking the lens at a fixed focal length improved my chances overall, due to steadier panning, but in bad light it was still a struggle.

I finally took the long awaited plunge and purchased the Canon 300mm f/2.8 L IS lens along with the 1.4x extender and 2x extender. My Bushhawk is still used despite the sometimes cumbersome weight, but this is the best setup for me with pin-sharp images almost every time in varied light conditions.

Listening to air-band radios has always been a long interest of mine (I own nine radios), and can, depending on which valley location has been chosen, give prior warning of aircraft that could be heading my way. This can add a different edge of excitement as I tend to be that bit more alert for the next few minutes, rather than if something just appeared in the valley without any warning.

In some valleys I have been to there's barely enough time to raise the camera to start shooting the subject, as the aircraft are upon you almost instantly with little or no warning at all. This pushes the excitement level to the maximum, which certainly makes for some dramatic shots if you're quick enough. So a 'heads-up' from the radios in those circumstances can greatly assist.

In one particular bizarre instance a two-second garbled transmission was all that was received on the radio. The background noise on the frequency indicated to me that it was a transmission from a Tornado GR4 and that there was at least a pair of them nearby at low level. A scan of frequencies on my other radio quickly located their chat frequency, which confirmed the aircraft types, which squadron they were flying with and also which air base they were from – two minutes later the two Tornados came roaring through the valley.

This is just one of many unusual examples I have witnessed from pursuing the hobby, which has certainly been very varied and memorable: from catching rare foreign aircraft, to having the only aircraft of the day come through within a thirty minute window of bright sunlight, having waited around for eight hours in less than average weather. Also witnessing a lightning bolt hit the valley floor right in front of me whilst on the mountainside, while sheltering under an umbrella from the torrential rain

With an acknowledging glance from the pilot on a solo sortie from RAF Valley, Hawk T1 XX156, 208 (R) Squadron, climbs through Bwlch Oerddrws on a bright 2 March 2010. To the credit of RAF Valley and RAF Leeming, none of the aircraft going the wrong way were Hawks. *Canon 40D; 400mm, 1/500 sec at f/8.0, ISO 400. (Photo by Michael Leek)*

Above: Clearing The Exit, after Bwlch Oerddrws, the student pilot checks for an inbound aircraft that could be coming to join The Mach Loop from the direction of Bala. This is Hawk T1A XX230, 19 (R) Squadron, on 17 December 2008. *Canon 40D; 420mm, 1/400 sec at f/4.0, ISO 500. (Photo by Michael Leek)*

Opposite Top: A Red Arrow, XX244, is caught passing a hill known to the low-flying photography fraternity as Bluebell, a few miles west of Dinas Mawddwy on the The Mach Loop, in mid-Wales. This was taken on 20 July 2012, when it was a bright and clear morning. *Nikon D300; 300mm, 1/1250 at f/4.5, ISO 250. (Photo by Jamie Smith)*

Opposite Bottom: One of the joys of low-level photography is that you do not know what is going to turn up and on Friday 14 July 2006 the newly-painted Hawk 120D demonstrator aircraft, ZJ951, was seen in The Mach Loop. Not visible in the photograph is another Hawk, flying above the demonstrator as a photo ship. This was the week leading up to the bi-annual Farnborough trade show and no doubt BAE Systems wanted publicity shots. The scheme chosen was similar to that used by the McLaren Formula 1 racing team. This aircraft subsequently became nicknamed 'The McLaren Hawk' by enthusiasts. *Canon 30D; 300 mm, 1/640 sec at f/7.1, ISO 250. (Photo by Brian Hodgson)*

(an event which the author can vouch for as he was there too). And even seeing a civilian light aircraft crash land into a tree on a hillside a couple of miles away from where I was positioned.

The list goes on …

Finally, being able to spend the day looking at some stunning scenery, at remote places I would have little need to go to, were it not for the hobby, is definitely worthwhile. In certain respects the scenic view might be the only thing I see all day.

Brian Hodgson
www.flickr.com/photos/churchward1956/

My interest in aviation started way back in 1968 when at school, and steam trains disappeared from our railways and their diesel replacements failed to ignite my interest in the same way as steam had. Some friends at school were into aircraft and so I started collecting aircraft numbers at my local Speke Airport in Liverpool (now Liverpool John Lennon).

I was quite happy with civil registrations and although Speke was not a busy airport I did get to see what would now be considered classic aircraft on day-to-day operations such as the Viscount, Airspeed Ambassador, Douglas DC-3, DC-4, DC-6, Bristol Britannia, BAC 111 and so on. Military aircraft did visit Speke and Army Beaver AL1s and Sioux AH1s (Bell 47G) would regularly stop off on the way to Northern Ireland. The large US Army storage depot at Burtonwood would bring in regular flights of Beech U-8F and U-8D Seminole aircraft, along with Convair C-131 Samaritans from the USAF. These military aircraft seemed mysterious as each air arm seemed to have its own numbering system but with the absence of a spotter's book at the time interest in military aircraft did not take off.

In the early 1970s this changed when I got to see military aircraft in action at a couple of air displays at Liverpool Airport. Two memories stand out: firstly, the sight and sound of Mosquito T3 RR299 skimming the rooftops over our house in its pre-display practice; I had not seen anything that low and fast before and to this day the Mosquito remains my favourite Second World War aircraft. Sadly RR299 was to crash on 21 July 1996, after a display at Barton in Lancashire.

The second memory was to witness an English Electric Lightning performing one of the type's legendary take-offs. The weather was glorious with deep blue skies and hot sun, the aircraft was an overall natural metal Lightning in 111 Squadron markings. The take-off with full afterburner was noisy. It had barely got airborne when the undercarriage was retracted, but it did not climb – instead it remained low until the end of the runway when, seeming to turn on a sixpence, it went vertical and continued to climb and climb until it was just a silver dot in the blue sky. It certainly impressed a spotty teenager and since that day it has been my favourite jet aircraft. I have seen many similar climb outs, recently from F15s and Typhoons, but they have not matched the Lightning.

Besides collecting the numbers, I wanted to take some photographs and Dad gave me his box camera. This took 120 roll film and, if you were careful when loading the camera, eight shots could be had from a roll of film. I used to develop the film and make prints during lunchtimes at school. The camera had two focus settings, portrait and scenic, with just one exposure setting; the viewfinder was tiny and had the image upside down, but I still got some shots and I developed them myself which gave me a lot of satisfaction. Next was a 126 roll film camera by, I think, Halina. I only had this a little while when I was able to buy a Zenith B SLR from money saved up from working as a car park attendant at Liverpool Airport.

Although it lacked facilities that we take for granted nowadays, the Zenith B was a good introduction to photography. It was manual focus, you had to use a separate light meter (the Leningrad 4 in my case, which I still have) and you had to manually stop down the lens. The procedure for taking a photograph was to take a light meter reading, then, depending on the speed of the film being used, work out the correct aperture and shutter speed combination, set the shutter speed and aperture on the camera, focus on the subject, stop down the lens to the selected aperture and then you could take the photograph. Cumbersome enough for a static subject but very difficult to use on a moving subject; for these the only way was to pre-focus on a spot on the taxiway or runway and get everything ready so that when the aircraft came by your pre-focused location you could get the aircraft in focus and just hope that the lighting conditions hadn't changed since you took the meter reading. The main skill in this process was correctly guessing at which point on the taxiway/runway the aircraft would fill the frame; quite often the guess was wrong and the frame was overfilled or the aircraft was too small. Still, I was able occasionally to get some half-decent shots.

The Zenith was to last me through university but on starting work I wanted something a lot better. I saved up my first wage packets, studied the camera magazines and took the plunge and purchased a Canon A1, with 50mm f1.8 lens, in 1981. The reason for choosing Canon, over any other make, was that they seemed to be the only manufacturer at that time,

Taken from Bwlch Oerddrws, Hawk T1 XX157, 208 (R) Squadron, making an aggressive turn out of the pass towards Bala on 30 July 2007.
Nikon D200; 300mm, 1/800 sec at f/5.3, ISO 400. (Photo by Meirion Williams)

Above: Mid-afternoon on 24 November 2009 sees Hawk T1A XX287, 19 (R) Squadron, on finals into RAF Kinloss, which is now closed (along with its Nimrod aircraft, thereby leaving Britain without any maritime patrol aircraft for the first time since before the Second World War). This photo has been processed using HDR software. *Canon 40D; 190mm, 1/160 sec at f/5.0, ISO 400. (Photo by Michael Leek)*

Opposite Top: The bi-annual NATO exercise JOINT WARRIOR provides opportunities to photograph Hawks operating out of RAF Lossiemouth. Here Hawk T1A XX285, 100 Squadron, RAF Leeming, is about to touch down on runway 05, in late-afternoon autumnal light on 10 October 2012. *Canon 40D; 300mm, 1/800 sec at f/2.8, ISO 400. (Photo by Michael Leek)*

Opposite Bottom: Wet, windy and foggy weather might seem to predominate in the UK, but sometimes – just occasionally – these conditions can inadvertently help the photographer. Here Hawk T1A XX222, RAF Leeming, taxis to the runway at RAF Leuchars in Fife. This HDR image was taken on 17 March 2011. *Canon 7D; 135mm, 1/500 sec at f/5.0, ISO 400. (Photo by Michael Leek)*

and at my price point, which offered a shutter priority mode on their cameras, something I felt was essential for aviation photography.

The quality of the Canon over the Zenith was evident straight away. Photographs were now correctly exposed 99.9 per cent of the time and pin sharp and I didn't have to make an exposure reading or shut down the lens as the camera did those for me.

Whilst reading the photography magazines back in 1980 one piece of advice was evident and is still true today: always buy the best lenses you can afford as the camera can only record what the lens presents to it. A poor lens on an expensive camera body is unlikely to provide a better image than a good lens on a cheaper body and more often than not it is the other way round with the cheaper camera and expensive lens providing the better image. With this in mind, over time, I gradually added Canon prime lenses at 35mm, 100mm and 200mm, and added a second body with the Canon T70.

With a full-time job, a marriage and a family, any aviation interest was limited mainly to air shows in the UK, although in the 1980s and 90s there were plenty to choose from and in June/July each year there seemed to be a show on nearly every weekend.

After Canon introduced the EF mount and autofocus in 1987, for the next few years there were plenty of second-hand camera bodies and lenses on sale as people traded in their FD mount lenses and cameras for the new EF mount and I added a Canon T90 and prime lenses at 24mm, 28mm, 135mm and 300mm to the, now bigger, camera bag. I stopped worrying about the serials of the aircraft and concentrated on getting better photographs and, as a result, I have enjoyed the hobby more since doing so.

I was quite happy with my manual focus cameras and lenses until 1999 when I saw some photographs taken on a Canon EF body and some of their expensive L-series lenses. These were of flying aircraft, rather than of static or taxiing aircraft and were showing a more dynamic image of the aircraft, than I was able to capture at the time. They were also consistently sharp, which can be difficult to achieve with a manual focus camera. So it was time to start saving again and, with the help of an end-of-year bonus, I was able to take the plunge and purchase a Canon EOS 5 and 28-135mm F3.5-5.6 IS and 100-400mm f4.5-f5.6L IS lenses.

Although I departed from using primes, both these lenses gave very good results on a film camera and the zoom range was ideal for going to an air show or visiting a base. The camera bag became a bit smaller as well. In the next few years I added a Canon EOS3 body and a 300mm f4L IS prime lens.

With the ending of the Cold War the number of air shows has reduced and the opportunities for getting some dynamic shots of aircraft were getting smaller. It is all very well getting a shot of an aircraft in the air but it doesn't always give an indication of speed unless the aircraft is generating some vapour. I also like getting shots of the topsides of aircraft which wasn't always possible at air shows as the aircraft were usually too far away or you were facing the sun.

I'd seen aircraft flitting in and out the valleys of the Lake District whilst on holiday and saw some pictures of low-flying aircraft on the internet; these seemed to be the sort of shot I was after. There were topsides galore and with the aircraft being below you there was land in the background; I wanted to get similar shots and began to research where I could see these aircraft.

In 2002 I had my first trip to the hills to the M6 pass at Tebay but it did not work out too well. I did not take into account how fast the aircraft would be travelling (fast jets usually between 400 to 500mph) and how small they would be in the frame on a full-frame film camera. Due to work commitments, I was not able to try my hand at low-level aircraft photography again until the summer of 2003 when I was made redundant and became self-employed, which meant I could plan my work and leisure time better. In the meantime digital cameras were now becoming affordable with a sensible number of pixels and in July 2003 I took the plunge and bought a Canon EOS 10D digital SLR. This had, what seemed at the time, a generous, 6 million pixels and a crop factor of 1.6 times which made my 300mm lens the equivalent of a 480mm on a 35mm full-frame camera. The camera seemed tailor-made to my requirements. Furthermore, I was no longer at the mercy of the photo processors who didn't seem to care about my prints, or to Kodak who over the years have lost and scratched my slide films. I was now in control; I did the processing.

My second trip out to try low level was to Wales and The Mach Loop. I went to the Tal-y-Llyn Pass at the narrowest point. It wasn't a busy day but seeing aircraft negotiate that pass had me hooked. From then on I wanted to try the low level as often as I could and in the next four or five years I went in search of low-level aircraft all over the UK whenever I had the time and the weather played ball. It is not just the photographs of the aircraft that thrill me, but also just seeing them fly below you, particularly after all those years of having to look up at them.

Apart from photographing the aircraft as they fly below you, I have been lucky enough to meet fellow photographers up on the hills and make new friends. There is often time for a good chat between aircraft movements and it is a relaxing way to spend

On a bitterly cold day on 2 February 2012, Hawk T1A XX199, from 208(R) Squadron, lines itself up to enter the Bwlch Llyn Bach pass in The Mach Loop, mid-Wales. This view enables us to see a typical Hawk T1A set up with a 30mm Aden cannon on the centreline and CBLS-100 practice-bomb carriers on each wing. On 13 December 2012 208 (R) Squadron used the Aden cannon for the last time. *Canon 7D; 300mm, 1/400 sec at f/2.8, ISO 400. (Photo by Brian Hodgson)*

Above: Hawk T1 XX220 from 208 (R) Squadron speeds through the Thirlmere valley in the Lake District on 31 March 2008. The line and height flown by the aircrew briefly enables the photographer to capture vehicles travelling along the road on the opposite side of the valley. This certainly adds to the feel of the aircraft flying low when other objects in the background can be seen like this. *Canon 30D; 400mm, 1/500 sec at f/5.6, ISO400. (Photo by Graham Farish)*

Opposite Top: In this interior shot taken at RAF Valley, on 25 June 2012, Hawk T2 ZK020, IV Squadron (R), is shown on jacks for servicing. Note the exceptionally clean hangar floor and tidy arrangement of equipment; these are safety requirements as any foreign object that gets into an aircraft prior to and during a flight could be dangerous. *Nikon D300; 50mm, 1/25 sec at f/3.5, ISO 200. (Photo by Meirion Williams)*

Opposite Bottom: With ZK035 devoid of any squadron markings, the Hawk T2 is seen taxiing across the runway at RAF Fairford on one of the arrival days for the annual Royal International Air Tattoo (RIAT) on 14 July 2011. At this time the Hawk T2s were being operated by 19 (R) Squadron, evidenced by the squadron colours on the visor cover of the pilot in the instructor's seat, but the aircraft were never to receive these markings. Instead, the Hawk T2s would take up the markings of IV Squadron after that squadron was disbanded following the ill-considered retirement of the Harrier from RAF service. *Canon 7D; 300mm, 1/640 sec at f/8.9, ISO 250. (Photo by Brian Hodgson)*

Above: Hawk T1A XX342, from the Empire Test Pilots School (ETPS) at MoD Boscombe Down, is seen performing touch-and-goes at nearby RNAS Yeovilton on 21 June 2010. At one time there were four Hawk T1s painted in one variation or another of this attractive, high visibility scheme, nicknamed 'Raspberry Ripple' by enthusiasts, but with two aircraft crashing (XX343 and XX344) and the ASTRA (Advanced Stability Training Aircraft), XX341, being repainted in the standard black scheme in 2005, this aircraft was the last Hawk to carry these colours. *Canon 7D; 200mm, 1/400 sec at f/11, ISO 200. (Photo by Brian Hodgson)*

Opposite Top: On a beautiful day in July 2007 at Bwlch Oerddrws in The Mach Loop, an Indian Air Force Hawk Mk 132 makes a low pass. This particular airframe is still in primer colours, being on a test flight from BAE Systems' airfield at Warton, Lancashire. Hawk Mk 132s eventually entered Indian Air Force service on 18 February 2008. *Canon 350D; 200mm, 1/640 sec at f/8.0, ISO 200. (Photo by Michael Leek)*

Opposite Bottom: A close-up from above of the cockpit of Hawk T1A XX185, 208 (R) Squadron, as it banks hard to port. Taken as the aircraft went through Bwlch Oerddrws on 9 October 2008. *Canon 40D; 300mm, 1/800 sec at f/7.1, ISO 400. (Photo by Michael Leek)*

Above: Here two Royal Navy pilots take their Hawk T1, XX217, in the markings of 208 (R) Squadron, on a straight and level path through The Mach Loop in mid-Wales, on 4 June, 2009. *Canon 40D; 420mm, 1/800 sec at f/7.1, ISO 400. (Photo by Michael Leek)*

Opposite Top: Captured going through Bwlch Oerddrws is Hawk T2 ZK018, IV Squadron, RAF Valley. This was taken on 19 October 2012. *Nikon D300; 300mm, 1/640 sec at f/2.8, ISO 200. (Photo by Meirion Williams)*

Opposite Bottom: A beautiful sunlit portrait of Hawk T2 ZK010, IV Squadron (R), RAF Valley, on a regular training sortie out of RAF Valley, Isle of Anglesey, as it traverses the The Mach Loop in mid-Wales. This was taken from Bluebell, west of the village of Dinas Mawddwy. This was shot early on the afternoon of 28 March 2012. *Nikon D300; 300mm, 1/1250 sec at f/4, ISO 250. (Photo by Jamie Smith)*

Above: With Lake District crags forming the backdrop, the Red Arrows get ready to perform at the Windermere air show on 24 July 2011. Sadly 2011 ended up being a tragic year for the team. On 20 August 2011 Flt Lt Jon Egging RAF was killed when his Hawk T1 crashed near Bournemouth airport whilst performing the airfield break to land. On 8 November 2011 Flt Lt Sean Cunningham RAF was killed whilst his Hawk T1 was stationary and on the ground, when the Martin Baker Mk 10 ejector seat fired but the parachute failed to deploy. This last accident resulted in the temporary grounding of all RAF Hawk and Tornado aircraft (both use the Mk 10 ejector seat) until the seats had been checked. With the loss of two experienced team members the routine for 2012 was cut down to seven aircraft, but returned to the full complement of nine aircraft for the 2013 season. *Canon 7D; 300mm, 1/1000 sec at f/8.0, ISO 250. (Photo by Brian Hodgson)*

Opposite Top: A perfect profile, in excellent winter afternoon light, of Hawk T1A XX158, 19 (R) Squadron, as it passes The Exit in The Mach Loop on 25 November 2008. *Canon 40D; 300mm, 1/500 sec at f/7.1, ISO 400. (Photo by Michael Leek)*

Opposite Bottom: Cockpit close-up of an unidentified Hawk T1 from 208 (R) Squadron, RAF Valley, as it heads through Cad East on 12 December 2007. *Canon 40D; 600mm, 1/1000 sec at f/5.6, ISO 500. (Photo by Michael Leek)*

a day. This has led to aviation trips overseas to France, Germany, Switzerland and Norway, and has reinvigorated my interest in aviation. Nowadays I enjoy visiting airfields and air shows just as much as heading up into the hills.

Alexander Klingelhöller
www.earth-and-sky.de

Even as a child I was fascinated by flying. In my youth, I built a large number of aircraft and helicopter models. In the region of my home I was surrounded by several military airfields, Laupheim, Memmingen and Leipheim, so I found continuing inspiration in the skies for my hobby.

During my military service with the Bundeswehr (German Army) in 1993 and 1994, and specifically with army aviation in Laupheim, I had the opportunity to take numerous flights on such helicopters as the BO-105, CH-53 and the Bell UH-1D. My job in the army was responsibility for the extension of the pilots' licences. At other times I was an observer on some of the helicopters. As an observer my task was to monitor the airspace during the flight, particularly on training flights for new pilots; as the instructor focused heavily on the training with the student, another observer during the flight was very helpful and useful. This resulted in me developing very good contacts with the aircrew and airborne troops that I maintain to this day.

During this period of military service my interest in photography grew, which was then still completely analogue. My first camera was a Pentax Z-70.

Since 2009, I have had my own website on which I've created a number of galleries in which I display photos taken at air-meets, airports and air shows. Through my press tours I have visited many airports and military stations across Europe, including Switzerland, Holland, Scotland, Italy, Austria, France and many more. My interests are not restricted to merely recording the aircraft, but include the 'look', or setting – what's behind the scenes of each squadron. This includes not only the technology but also the missions, the training and the people. My images and text are frequently used by the aviation press, such as *Flieger Revue* (www.fliegerrevue.de), *Combat Aircraft* (www.combataircraft.com), *Scale Edition* (http://www.vth.de), the *Rotorblatt* (www.rotorblatt.de), and many more.

In addition, I have designed photo books about my aviation interests. These photo books cover shooting at Axalp in the Swiss mountains, the NATO Tiger Meet and the historic aircraft meeting at Hahnweide, not far from Stuttgart. Readers may access these books through my website at http://neu.earth-and-sky.de/shop.html

My photographic equipment consists of a Canon 5D Mark III, Canon 7D and lenses 24-105 F4, 70-200 F2, 8 and 100-400 F 4.5-5.6

The pictures in this book were made with my previous Sony equipment, which consisted of a Sony Alpha 700 and a 70-400 f3.5-5.6 lens.

I work for a major German pharmaceutical company. I'm married with two children – and my son shares my passion for flying and has been with me on numerous visits to military airfields.

Michael Leek
www.aviagraphica.co.uk and www.michaelleek.co.uk

My interest in the technological development of military aircraft started by living relatively close to the famous RAF Biggin Hill, having unlimited access to the unique collection of Second World War aircraft that were housed there in the 1960s, and the books by the late William Green. I should also mention my passion for the Hawker Hunter and the BAC TSR2. I was a frequent visitor to many air shows (I rarely go now because of the restrictions on flying displays). Now, even with a much smaller RAF, it's through digital photography that my interest in military aviation continues.

'Military' experience, such as it was, was through brief membership of the Air Training Corps – but they wouldn't let me fly within three months of joining so I resigned. Then followed a few years with the Sea Cadet Corps, joining a landlocked unit in south London, although we did have our own ex-naval launch on the Thames, even if it did struggle to stay afloat. Many years later, I spent ten years with the now defunct Royal Naval Auxiliary Service (RNXS). The RNXS was the result of the Cold War and gave civilian volunteers – aka cheerful reprobates, from all walks of life – the opportunity to spend time at sea on fleet tenders and ex-minesweepers. The sea-going element of the RNXS is best described as 'Dad's Army at Sea' although without weapons training (we remained civilians even in uniform). However, seamanship and navigation were taught to the high standards of the RN, which was thorough and stood me in good stead on many occasions, including a single-handed voyage in the Mediterranean.

Because of my interest in how things work I went to Ravensbourne College of Art and Design to train as an illustrator. This included film-based photography (as a tool for reference purposes). On graduating I entered professional practice, working for book and magazine publishers, the MoD, and for the aircraft industries

The Hawk T1 might not be the front-line fast jet that's preferred by amateur photographers when in the hills, but there's no denying that it does have graceful lines, from any angle. Indeed, the Hawk has a strong pedigree, not least the equally graceful lines of that other great Hawker aircraft, the Hunter – also considered a pilot's aeroplane. Here an unidentified Hawk T1 from 208 (R) Squadron, RAF Valley, makes a pleasing pass through Cad West on a damp, grey day on 23 July 2007. *Canon 40D; 300mm, 1/1250 sec at f/5.0, ISO 320. (Photo by Michael Leek)*

Above: Turning onto runway 05 at RAF Lossiemouth for a JOINT WARRIOR exercise sortie is this Hawk T1A XX189 of 100 Squadron. This was taken on 10 October 2012 in excellent late afternoon light. *Canon 7D; 200mm, 1/800 sec at f/9.0, ISO 320. (Photo by Michael Leek)*

Opposite Top: With a wave from the instructor in the back seat, Hawk T1 XX174, 208 (R) Squadron, makes a straight and level pass through Bwlch Oerddrws in The Mach Loop. This was taken on 30 May 2008. *Canon 40D; 420mm, 1/640 sec at f/4.0, ISO 500. (Photo by Michael Leek)*

Opposite Bottom: In this close-up photograph of Hawk T1 XX175, 208 (R) Squadron, the instructor in the back seat has control as the aircraft banks through Bwlch Oerddrws on 16 October 2008. *Canon 40D; 300mm, 1/800 sec at f/4.5, ISO 400. (Photo by Michael Leek)*

Above: In this shot, taken on a very wet day at RAF Valley, Hawk T2 ZK020 is caught taxiing back to the ramp after returning from a photo shoot at RAF Marham, Norfolk, on 15 June 2012. The photo shoot was specifically for squadron special or anniversary tail markings. *Nikon D300; 100mm, 1/1000 sec at f/4.8, ISO 400. (Photo by Meirion Williams)*

Opposite Top: A pairs take-off from a grey and damp RAF Leuchars by Hawk T1 XX245, 208 (R) Squadron, and Hawk T1A XX325, also from 208 (R) Squadron, the latter wearing its 2008 display markings, on 13 September 2008. The pilot of the second aircraft, on the right, is Flt Lt Dave Davies. *Canon 40D; 100mm, 1/250 sec at f/9.0, ISO 400. (Photo by Michael Leek)*

Opposite Bottom: An impressive HDR photograph of Hawk T1A XX165, from 208 (R) Squadron, as it banks to port through Bwlch Oerddrws on 9 October 2008. *Canon 40D; 300mm, 1/800 sec at f/4.0, ISO 400. (Photo by Michael Leek)*

Above: In this HDR image Hawk T1A XX331, 100 Squadron, RAF Leeming, rotates through the grey mist as it departs from RAF Leuchars on 13 September 2008. *Canon 40D; 200mm, 1/160 sec at f/13, ISO 500. (Photo by Michael Leek)*

Opposite Top: A 'classic' view of a British Aerospace Hawk T1 as it works its way through The Mach Loop in Wales. In this example, Hawk T1W XX313, 208 (R) Squadron, on a solo sortie, pulls up and banks to port heading for the Cadair Idris pass. This was taken on a relatively clear day on 12 December 2007. *Canon 40D; 300mm, 1/1250 sec at f/3.5, ISO 200. (Photo by Michael Leek)*

Opposite Bottom: The late-afternoon winter sunshine casts an unusual shadow below 208 (R) Squadron's Hawk T1A XX201 as it passes through Bwlch Oerddrws in The Mach Loop on 9 November 2006. The unusual lighting gives the illusion that the Hawk is skimming along the surface of the hill opposite but in reality it was a good 300 feet above the ground. *Canon 30D; 300mm, 1/640 sec at f/9.0, ISO 400. (Photo by Brian Hodgson)*

Above: On a glorious 13 December 2007, Hawk T1 XX156, 208 (R) Squadron, contrasts well against the brightly sunlit background. *Canon 40D; 300mm, 1/500 sec at f/4.5, ISO 200. (Photo by Michael Leek)*

Opposite Top: Flying through a cross wind, an unidentified Hawk T1 from 208 (R) Squadron is caught on finals into RAF Lossiemouth. This HDR image was taken 17 March 2010. *Canon 7D; 400mm, 1/1250 sec at f/9.0, ISO 320. (Photo by Michael Leek)*

Opposite Bottom: Piloted by the instructor in the back seat, as the student keeps his hands raised to indicate he's not touching any controls, this Hawk T1W, XX201 of 208 (R) Squadron, navigates through Bwlch Oerddrws on a sunny 16 September 2009. *Canon 40D; 300mm, 1/1000 sec at f/5.6, ISO 400. (Photo by Michael Leek)*

in the UK (including Concorde), The Netherlands and Germany (where I worked on the now retired VFW-614 and on the first Airbus, the A300). I've been commissioned to produce paintings of the Lancaster, Spitfire, Hunter, Lightning and Phantom, mainly for retired RAF aircrew.

My visual arts career included many years at the Arts University Bournemouth, where I became Head of the School of Illustration. I completed postgraduate teacher training at Bournemouth University, an MA (Visual Arts Practice, Education and Management) at Middlesex University, and an MPhil ('The History and Application of Information Illustration through the Development of Naval Architecture') at the Royal College of Art. I'm a member of a number of historical societies and a Life Fellow of the Royal Society of Arts.

During my career in design education, I designed and managed a number of aviation-related projects for the RAF (including The RAF Vulcan Display Team), the Fleet Air Arm Museum, the Imperial War Museum, and the Science Museum.

I left design education in 2008 to pursue my own work, and now devote my time to illustration, photography and editorial work.

My book, *Military Low Flying in the UK*, also published by Pen and Sword Books, February 2012, was the *first* book to be published anywhere on the subject of low flying.

Reflecting my interests in maritime history and model making, I was, for a number of years, assistant editor of the quarterly journal *Model Shipwright*, and of the first annual publication *Shipwright*.

I've been fortunate in having had some of my aviation photographs published in *Air Forces Monthly*, *Flight International*, *RAF News*, *Aircraft Illustrated*, *Amateur Photographer*, *Practical Photography*, *Photography Monthly*, *The Daily Mail*, *The Northern Scot*, *The Press & Journal*, the RAF Museum and elsewhere. I've also been twice Featured Photographer with Flight Global/*Flight International*, and was a runner-up in the Action category of the annual *Photographer of the Year* competition run by *Practical Photography* magazine.

Jamie Smith
www.jmsphotos.co.uk

Professionally, I couldn't be further removed from military aviation photography: I'm a self-employed gardener. I live on the lovely rural Wiltshire-Dorset border, surrounded by gently rolling hills over which there are some great walks and opportunities for landscape photography, two of the ways in which I like to unwind. My walks in the hills around my

home and much further afield – such as the Lake District and Scotland – combined with my interest in photography led me to low-flying military aviation photography.

It was in 1996 during a walking holiday in the Scottish Highlands that I heard a low, distant rumble. In no time at all a military jet flew past me, seemingly hugging the contours of the hills. From the ridge I was on I had a perfect view. The excitement made me vow to try to capture such an event on film. At the time, a mere teenager, I was already familiar with camcorders, so still photography was not much of a step.

Since that memorable occasion I've been completely hooked on all kinds of military aircraft photography, from helicopters to troop carriers. However, the ultimate has, and always will be, aircraft training low level through the Welsh mountains, particularly through The Mach Loop. The first time I took a photograph of a low-flying aircraft was in Wales in February 2008. I've never looked back as they say. Now I travel up to Wales as often as I can, hoping not just for the norm, but also for the unexpected or the unusual, be it an aircraft or its angle of attack as flies through the valleys. I do not restrict myself to Wales, but also visit my own local region, such as Salisbury Plain where I've been successful capturing helicopters working with ground troops.

I started with Canon but eventually moved to Nikon. I now have a Nikon D300 with relevant Nikon lenses, including a 300mm f/2.8 prime that's ideal for low level, particularly in Wales. I take my camera kit with me whenever possible and in recent years I've extended my choice of locations by visiting Norway and France, the latter to capture French military aircraft training low level (which I did with Brian Hodgson, another contributor to this book – together we're probably the first amateur photographers to visit France specifically for low-flying photography).

In some respects I see myself as recording a small piece of aviation history as so many aircraft have been retired earlier than planned, leaving the skies over the UK much emptier than they were even a few years ago.

A real bonus with this type of photography is the people you meet, many of whom become good friends, the common interest being a good starting point.

Meirion Williams
I'm a retired Leading Ambulance Technician from the Welsh Ambulance Service, based at Barmouth, on the coast of mid-Wales. I served for twenty-six years and before that I worked as a plasterer and slater.

Hawk T2 ZK011, in full IV Squadron (R) markings and coded 'B', is seen leaving Bwlch Oerddrws in The Mach Loop on 10 December 2012. Fortunately for the photographer, the aircraft has caught the sunlight even though there was plenty of cloud around, as evidenced by the patches of shadow on the hills opposite. Note the missile rails are painted white in this instance whereas they are normally black. The two practice missile rounds that are carried enable the acquisition of targets in the cockpit and so help simulate the realities of air-to-air combat. *Canon 7D; 300mm, 1/800 sec at f/4.0, ISO 100. (Photo by Brian Hodgson)*

Above: It must be quite a milestone in the training of a fast-jet pilot when he or she has reached the stage in their training where they take a fast jet on their first solo sortie. Here a student from 208 (R) Squadron, in Hawk T1 XX231, is caught going straight and level through Bwlch Oerddrws. This was taken on 30 May 2008. *Canon 40D; 420mm, 1/1000 sec at f/4.0, ISO 500. (Photo by Michael Leek)*

Opposite Top: Making a pleasing and contrasting sight is Red Arrow Hawk T1 XX308, RAF Scampton, as it goes through Bwlch Oerddrws on a low sortie on 20 July 2012. *Nikon D300; 300mm, 1/500 sec at f/2.8, ISO 200. (Photo by Meirion Williams)*

Opposite Bottom: Still carrying the special marks applied for the 2006 air show season, Hawk T1 XX159 is seen in The Mach Loop in the Snowdonia National Park, on 11 April 2007. The 2006 scheme celebrated the eighty-fifth anniversary of No. 4 Flying Training School (FTS) as well as one million RAF flying hours in the type. Although special marks are applied to aircraft for display at air shows, these aircraft are still used in normal day-to-day flying tasks when not being displayed. Whilst low-level flying is avoided during the air show season, due to the risk of bird strikes ruining an expensive paint scheme, once the season is over then such restrictions may be removed. *Canon 30D; 300mm, 1/1000 sec at f/5.0, ISO 200. (Photo by Brian Hodgson)*

Above: A welcome feature of the modern UK armed forces is the increasing role played by women and this was recognized in 2011 with the solo Hawk display pilot being Flt Lt Juliette (Jules) Fleming from 208 (R) Squadron. The scheme chosen for 2011 celebrated the seventieth anniversary of RAF Valley, Isle of Anglesey, Wales. As usual, two Hawk aircraft, XX244 and XX245, were painted in this special scheme. XX244 is seen landing at RAF Fairford for the 2011 Royal International Air Tattoo. *Canon 50D; 200mm, 1/400 sec at f/9.0, ISO 200. (Photo by Brian Hodgson)*

Opposite Top: Another classic view of an unidentified Hawk T1 from 208 (R) Squadron as it banks to starboard for its approach through the Cadair Idris pass in The Mach Loop on 23 July 2008. *Canon 40D; 300mm, 1/250 sec at f/6.3, ISO 320. (Photo by Michael Leek)*

Opposite Bottom: Another shot of an Indian Air Force Hawk Mk 132, ZK125, as it goes through Bwlch Oerddrws on 30 July 2007. The aircraft, on a test flight from BAE Systems, Warton, is still in primer colours and temporary UK military aircraft markings. *Nikon D200; 300mm, 1/500 sec at f/9.0, ISO 400. (Photo by Meirion Williams)*

Above: Again showing off the clean lines of the British Aerospace Hawk through The Mach Loop is Hawk T1A XX263, 208 (R) Squadron, from RAF Valley. This was taken on 29 May 2008. *Canon 40D; 420mm, 1/1250 sec at f/4.0, ISO 400. (Photo by Michael Leek)*

Opposite Top: With the sun having hardly risen and frost still on the hills, Hawk T2 ZK010, in IV Squadron (R) markings and coded 'A', is seen in The Mach Loop in the Snowdonia National Park, mid-Wales, on 29 November 2012. *Canon 7D; 300 mm, 1/800 sec at f/3.5, ISO 160. (Photo by Brian Hodgson)*

Opposite Bottom: In 2004 the Indian Air Force (IAF) ordered sixty-six Hawk Mk 132 aircraft, with twenty-four being built in the UK and the remaining forty-two built by Hindustan Industries in India. The UK-built aircraft formed the basis for training IAF instructors in the UK prior to the introduction of the aircraft in the IAF in February 2008. Whilst the training was taking place in 2007 and 2008 the IAF Hawk Mk 132s were often seen flying low-level sorties in Wales and the Lake District National Park in England. The example pictured here, ZK121, was seen in The Mach Loop on 18 July 2007. In general, whilst performing training flights in the UK, the aircraft were still in the primer scheme with no IAF markings applied, but carrying a UK military serial and RAF roundels. ZK121 first flew on 11 December 2006 and was delivered to the IAF on 23 October 2009 with IAF serial A3480. *Canon 20D; 300mm, 1/640 sec at f/6.3, ISO 200. (Photo by Brian Hodgson)*

Above: A Royal Navy sub-lieutenant takes Hawk T1 XX245, 208 (R) Squadron, on a solo sortie through the Cadair Idris pass on a bright sunny morning on 24 October 2007. *Canon 40D; 375mm, 1/1250 sec at f/5.6, ISO 250. (Photo by Michael Leek)*

Opposite Top: The seventieth anniversary of RAF Valley, Isle of Anglesey, was commemorated with this specially-painted Hawk T1, XX245, seen here at an RAF Valley enthusiasts' day on 3 August 2011. This aircraft is usually attached to 208 (R) Squadron. *Nikon D300; 200mm, 1/500 sec at f/6.3, ISO 200. (Photo by Meirion Williams)*

Opposite Bottom: By spring 2012 many of the Hawk T2s were wearing IV (R) Squadron markings, and ZK010, the first of the Hawk T2s, is seen wearing the code 'A' on a low-level sortie through the Lake District in early May 2012. The Hawk T2 can carry two AIM-9L Sidewinder missiles on rails attached to the wing tips rather than on under wing pylons, as on the Hawk T1A. For training purposes real missiles are not carried but training versions that allow the telemetry to work so that they can be 'locked on' in a simulated scenario. *Canon 7D; 300mm, 1/800 sec at f/4.0, ISO 100. (Photo by Brian Hodgson)*

I've been interested in aviation since I was a small boy, and have always had a particular interest in military aircraft, going back to the mid-1950s. Being brought up not far from RAF Llanbedr, located in the Snowdonia National Park, near the village of Llanbedr, Gwynedd, in north-west Wales, probably contributed to my interest. It was then possible to see many different types of military aircraft operating out of the airfield before its closure as an RAF station in 1957 and its later closure as an RAE centre in 1992 (although it continued to operate as a defence test and evaluation centre until 2001).

My interest in photography came in the 35mm film days. My first camera was a Canon AE1, with manual focusing – which was a challenge when taking photos of fast jets as so many were out-of-focus, or I had inadvertently chopped off the nose, tail and/or wings. And you never knew you'd made these errors until after waiting a week for the prints to come back.

The change from Canon to Nikon came with, yet again, a film camera, a Nikon F60, then a Nikon 601, before my first digital camera. And what a transformation a Nikon D70 is to the present and earlier two Nikon digital bodies I have; a Nikon D200 and Nikon D300.

My lens kit includes a Nikon 28-80mm wide angle, Nikon 80-400mm and a Nikon 300mm 2.8 prime lens. These cover my needs for air shows and low-level photography.

As my main interest is in low-flying photography I'm lucky to be living in Barmouth, only thirty minutes away from one of the busiest designated low-flying areas in the UK, namely the almost famous Mach Loop. This is a very popular area with photographers from all over the world and I have been fortunate to have met people from as far away as Japan and Australia, and obviously from many European countries, making good friends with many of these like-minded amateurs.

However, The Mach Loop is not as busy in 2013 as it was in the past. This is the result of the standing down of so many squadrons because of government cuts to the number of aircraft in service, a far cry from the 'good old days' fifteen or sixteen years ago when it was possible to have up to fifty movements a day,. And even earlier, in the 1960s and 1970s, there were occasions when nearly a hundred movements were recorded in a single day over Dinas.

An occasion that stands out in particular, and which I will always remember, is witnessing a four- ship of RAF McDonnell-Douglas Phantom F4s tailing each other low through to Tal-y-Llyn (via what is known as Cad West). This was in the mid-1980s, but alas I had no camera. The moral of that is if you are in this area make sure a camera is ready as you never know what you could see.

This photo is just one example of many of what low-flying photography is about. It makes the long and sometimes difficult climb up a mountain, with a heavy bag full of camera equipment, food and waterproof clothing, worthwhile. It's also not unknown to spend up to eight or more hours and only have one aircraft go past and below you. Here Hawk T1W XX181, 208 (R) Squadron, RAF Valley, flies low over a winter landscape as it navigates through The Mach Loop on the morning of 10 February 2009. *Canon 40D; 300mm, 1/320 sec at f/7.1, ISO 400. (Photo by Michael Leek)*

Above: Here the student and instructor of Hawk T1 XX245, wearing the ninetieth anniversary markings of the RAF Benevolent Fund combined with a special scheme for the 2009 display season, acknowledges the photographer on its low-flying sortie through The Mach Loop. This was taken on 23 October 2009. *Nikon D300; 300mm, 1/500 sec at f/3.2, ISO 200. (Photo by Meirion Williams)*

Opposite Top: When the sun shines in the winter months the light can be magical, if you are prepared to suffer the cold, although there remains a risk of mist and fog lingering in the valleys when shooting low level. Most times the mist lifts, but often this is not the case and a frustrating day is the result. In the distance can be seen mist and fog in the valleys but, fortunately for the photographer, it has cleared in The Mach Loop, enabling this portrait of 100 Squadron Hawk T1A XX236 to be captured on 9 January 2013. *Canon 7D; 300mm, 1/800 sec at f/5.6, ISO 160. (Photo by Brian Hodgson)*

Opposite Bottom: Photographing the specially-painted air show aircraft low level in the UK can be something of a lottery since during the air show season they are seldom seen low level due to the risk of a bird strike; the best chance is usually after the last show of the year. One of the 2006 air show Hawk T1s, XX195, is seen in the last light of a cold November day in 2006 exiting Bwlch Oerddrws in The Mach Loop in Wales on its way back to RAF Valley. The 2006 Hawk display pilot was Flt Lt Martin Pert. *Canon 30D; 300mm, 1/640 sec at f/3.2, ISO 400. (Photo by Brian Hodgson)*

Above: This 100 Squadron Hawk T1 is seen passing through the Lake District on 7 March 2007. Practice AIM-9L Sidewinder missiles are carried, a not uncommon sight for 100 Squadron Hawks. These practice missiles enable the acquisition of targets for a more realistic combat training environment in the cockpit. XX198 was delivered to the RAF on 3 April 1978 and so was nearly twenty-nine years old when this photograph was taken. It is still in service at the time of writing thus giving thirty-five years of useful service to the RAF – and good value for money to UK taxpayers. *Canon 30D; 300mm, 1/640 sec at f/4.0, ISO 200. (Photo by Brian Hodgson)*

Opposite Top: On a very misty, damp and dull afternoon on 13 September 2008, the season's display Hawk T1A, XX325, 208 (R) Squadron, rolls down the runway past the last airworthy Avro Vulcan B2 delta-wing bomber at RAF Leuchars, Fife. The pilot is Flt Lt Dave Davies. *Canon 40D; 200mm, 1/200 sec at f/10, ISO 500. (Photo by Michael Leek)*

Opposite Bottom: A pleasing early morning autumn shot of Royal Navy Hawk T1W XX224 as it goes through the Cadair Idris pass towards Tal-y-Llyn lake. This was taken on 24 October 2007. *Canon 40D; 400mm, 1/800 sec at f/5.6, ISO 400. (Photo by Michael Leek)*

Above: RAF Centre of Aviation's Hawk T1 XX327, MoD Boscombe Down, heads straight and level through Bwlch Oerddrws in the morning light of early autumn on 16 September 2009. *Canon 40D; 400mm, 1/800 sec at f/5.6, ISO 400. (Photo by Michael Leek)*

Opposite Top: With the autumn colours on the trees forming the backdrop, 208 (R) Squadron's Hawk T1A XX187, is seen in The Mach Loop in Wales on 25 October 2010. 208 Squadron's colours have been seen on Hawk aircraft since April 1994, after the squadron ceased flying the Buccaneer, when 234 (R) Squadron, attached to No. 4 Flying Training Squadron at RAF Valley, was re-badged as 208 (R) Squadron. *Canon 7D; 300mm, 1/800 sec at f/5.0, ISO 200. (Photo by Brian Hodgson)*

Opposite Bottom: The angle of attack of this Hawk T1, XX234, from 208 (R) Squadron, provides the photographer with a dramatic composition, the vapour pulling off the starboard wing adding to the sensation of speed. This photograph was taken at mid-day on 10 February 2009. *Canon 40D; 300mm, 1/320 sec at f/5.6, ISO 500. (Photo by Michael Leek)*

Above: With a wave from the back-seater, one of the two Hawk T1s operated for the RAF Centre of Aviation Medicine – in this case XX162 – runs through Bwlch Oerddrws in The Mach Loop, mid-afternoon on 29 May 2008. *Canon 40D; 300mm, 1/1000 sec at f/4.5, ISO 400. (Photo by Michael Leek)*

Opposite Top: Powering away from Bwlch Oerddrws towards The Exit is Hawk T1A XX185, from 208 (R) Squadron, on 9 October 2008. This is an HDR image. *Canon 40D; 300mm, 1/800 sec at f/4.5, ISO 400. (Photo by Michael Leek)*

Opposite Bottom: The Finnish Air Force ordered fifty Hawk Mk51s in 1978 with deliveries being made between December 1980 and September 1985. The first four aircraft were built in the UK with the remainder being assembled by Valton Lentokonetehdas in Finland. Seven additional aircraft were delivered in 1993-94 and these were designated Hawk Mk51A. Seen whilst on deployment to RAF Valley in September 2013 is HW-351 Hawk Mk50A of 41 Fighter Squadron, Finnish Air Force. *Canon 7D; 300mm, 1/800 sec at f/5.0, ISO 160. (Photo by Brian Hodgson)*

Appendix II

Bibliography and sources

The following is a list of all sources consulted in the writing and preparation of this book. Quality is variable, as is the extent and depth of material. Earlier books and articles (i.e. published before about 1995) tend to be more thorough in their coverage, whereas later publications possibly reflect the shorter attention span of readers, influenced, no doubt, by the Internet. This also applies to aviation magazines, particularly in the UK, where quality writing and in-depth articles are now rare (in comparison to articles published in the former *Flying Review International* and the technical articles for which *Flight International* is renowned). Today the apparent emphasis is on short, superficial articles and, in one particular example, the variable quality of the editor's personal photographs – often at the expense of far better contributions from readers, although at least one magazine is currently edited by a semi-professional aviation photographer.

The only relatively recent magazine that published quality, in-depth articles was the large format *World Air Power Journal* (1990-2000), but unfortunately this is no longer published. *World Air Power Journal* combined superb photography and technical illustrations with very thorough technical design, development and service histories of military aircraft, with each issue having a feature article on a specific aircraft.

Another problem with many military aviation magazines in the UK is that when it comes to reporting on matters relating to the RAF in particular and, in some respects, the USAF too, there is too much subjective reliance on blindly reporting the official line rather than present the information objectively and impartially, through informed analysis. Indeed, the author has been told that at some RAF stations operating the Typhoon the military aviation press are strictly controlled in case they talk to aircrew and discover facts that the MoD/RAF would rather not be in the public domain because it would show defects or failings in the operational capability of the aircraft. (An example of the operational shortcomings of the Typhoon was apparent during the NATO-led Operation UNIFIED PROTECTOR – Operation ELLAMY in the UK – over Libya in March 2011, in

support of United Nations Resolution 1973, when Typhoons were unable to operate in the ground attack role without the support of Tornado GR4s). How accurate this is cannot be confirmed, but it has a ring of truth about it when related to the flight testing of the Lockheed F-35 Lightning II where, for all its expensive technology and stealth capabilities, a major flaw in its design, as reported by the very experienced pilots on the flight test programme, is something as basic as the pilot's vision from the cockpit, which apparently is well below acceptable norms for a modern fast jet. Compare, for example, the excellent field of vision of the Hawk T1 and T2. I am sure the powers-that-be would have preferred this fact about the F-35 to have remained confidential considering the appalling and spiralling costs of this still questionable aircraft.

Even the current RAF *The Official Annual Review 2013*, or previous recent editions, do not compare with the RAF *Yearbooks* from the 1970s and 1980s, or even earlier. The *Review* is thin on substance, with jargon-rich interviews of serving personnel (making one question whether RAF officers actually talk like this in person). However, the photography is invariably of high quality. Furthermore, the former *Yearbooks* covered a balance of contemporary and current RAF matters with the historical, often with detailed cutaway line perspective illustrations, full colour profiles and good photography. Even though the *Yearbooks* from previous decades were published with the official sanction of the RAF (and therefore the MoD), the articles were well-researched, objective and impartial, and often challenging or questioning official defence policies, management and procurement decisions.

Finally, whilst my book *Military Low Flying in the UK* was the first book to be published on the photographing of military aircraft in a low-flying environment, specific mention must be made of a small, little-known booklet entitled *Lowdown*, by Andy Heap and Paul Jackson. This privately printed and circulated spiral-bound booklet was published in 1998. It gives summary details of low-flying areas in the UK and a complete list, current at the time of publication, of all UK ranges. The small selection of photographs

During the JOINT WARRIOR exercise held in October 2013, Iain Common and the author spent a few days high above Glen Tilt in Perthshire. On the day this photograph was taken it was extremely windy, with the occasional shower, and very quiet. However, we were eventually rewarded with a four-ship, in line ahead, of Hawks from 100 Squadron, RAF Leeming. Here Hawk T1A XX346, flies level with the author as it takes a straight path through the northern end of the glen before negotiating a number of tight S-bends. Because of these tight bends Glen Tilt is flowed from north to south. This was taken on 10 October 2013. *Canon 7D; 300mm, 1/1000 sec at f/9.0, ISO 400. (Photo by Michael Leek)*

Above: Passing over Grasmere in the Lake District, the Boscombe Down crew of this Hawk T2, ZK010, put the aircraft through its paces. This is one of the earliest flown Hawk T2s that was destined for the RAF and was eventually handed over to 19 (R) Squadron at RAF Valley once testing was complete. *Canon 30D; 400mm, 1/640 sec at f/7.1, ISO 200. (Photo by Graham Farish)*

Opposite Top: Taken from a location in The Mach Loop known as Bluebell, this Finnish Hawk Mk50, HW-355, was captured on a low-level sortie from RAF Valley during a two-week deployment to the RAF station. *Nikon D300; 300mm, 1/1250 sec at f/4.0, ISO 250. (Photo by Jamie Smith)*

Opposite Bottom: Sweeping low through the Thirlmere valley in the Lake District is Hawk Mk132 ZK142, from BAE Systems' complex at Warton in Lancashire. This is one of a batch of Hawks that was ordered by the Indian Air Force, with the BAe Systems crews testing each one in different flying roles before delivering them to the Indians. *Canon 30D; 400mm, 1/640 sec at f/8.0, ISO 200. (Photo by Graham Farish)*

show how much more varied the aircraft types were that used the UK low-flying system as relatively recently as only fifteen years ago. Unfortunately my copy was not acquired until after my low-flying book was published.

In addition to listing sources, I have tried to make this bibliography as comprehensive as possible. If any reader is aware of any omissions I would be grateful if they could let me know the details so that future editions of this book may be updated.

Aerospace, British, *British Aerospace Hawk Advanced trainer/ground attack aircraft: A Technical Description*, British Aerospace Weybridge Division, Weybridge, 1985.

——, *Hawk 200*, British Aerospace Weybridge Division, Weybridge, 1985.

Baker, Richard, *Red Arrows*, Dalton Watson Fine Books, 2005.

Bennett, Chris, *The Red Arrows*, Sutton Publishing Ltd, 2003.

Bonello, Michael & Caruana, Richard J. (eds), *The Red Arrows, Thirty Years of Brilliance*, Eclat Initiatives Ltd, 1994.

Braybrook, Roy, *British Aerospace Hawk*, Osprey, 1984.

Chesnau, Roger & Rimell, Raymond, *Aeroguide 1 - British Aerospace Hawk T Mk1*, Linewrights Ltd, 1983.

——, *British Aerospace Hawk T Mk1*, Pacific Aero Press, 1984.

Cooke, Gillian & Cooke, Richard, *The Red Arrows*, Virgin Books, 1987, 208p.

Cunnane, Tony, *The Inside Story: A Behind the Scenes look at the World's Premier Aerobatic Display Team*, Woodfield Publishing, 2002.

——, *Red Arrows: A Year in the Life of*, Andre Deutsch, 1997.

Cunnane, Tony, & Bennett, Chris; *Red Arrows*, Andre Deutsch Ltd, 1997.

Curtis, Howard J., *Military Aircraft Markings 2008*, Midland (Ian Allan Publishing), Hersham, 2008.

——, *Military Aircraft Markings 2009*, Midland (Ian Allan Publishing), Hersham, 2009.

——, *Military Aircraft Markings 2010*, Midland (Ian Allan Publishing), Hersham, 2010.

——, *Military Aircraft Markings 2011*, Midland (Ian Allan Publishing), Hersham, 2011.

——, *Military Aircraft Markings 2012*, Midland (Ian Allan Publishing), Hersham, 2012.

——, *Military Aircraft Markings 2013*, Ian Allan Publishing, Hersham, 2013.

Donald, David, *World Air Power Journal, Vol 22, Focus Aircraft: British Aerospace Hawk: Complete Analysis of Britain's Most Successful Aircraft of Recent Years*, Aerospace Publishing Ltd, 1995.

Eden, Paul J., & Moeng, Soph (eds), *Modern Military Aircraft Anatomy, Technical drawings of 118 Aircraft, 1945 to the present day*, Amber Books Ltd, London, 2002.

Eden, Paul E (ed), *Royal Air Force: The Official Annual Review 2013*, Key Publishing Ltd, Stamford, Lincolnshire, 2013.

English, Malcolm, *BAE Systems Hawk AJT*, Key Publishing Ltd (BAE Systems-*Air International*), 2007.

Evans, Andy, *BAE Systems Hawk: Reference Guide for Modellers and Enthusiasts*, SAM Publications, 2008.

Green, William, & Swanborough, Gordon (eds), *Royal Air Force Yearbook 1975*, Royal Air Force Benevolent Fund (RAFBF), London, 1975.

——, *Royal Air Force Yearbook 1976*, Royal Air Force Benevolent Fund (RAFBF), London, 1976, 68p.

——, *Royal Air Force Yearbook 1986*, Royal Air Force Benevolent Fund (RAFBF), London, 1986.

——, *Royal Air Force Yearbook 1987*, Royal Air Force Benevolent Fund (RAFBF), London, 1987.

Gunston, Bill (ed), *The Encyclopaedia of World Air Power*, London, 1981.

Heap, Andy, & Jackson, Paul, *Lowdown*, Tactical Publications (privately printed), 1998.

Hanna, Ray, *The Red Arrows*, Photo Precision Ltd, 1973.

Hunter, Jamie, *Fighting Force: 90th Anniversary of the Royal Air Force*, Touchstone Books Ltd, 2008.

——, *Red Arrows*, Touchstone Books Ltd, 2011.

IPC Business Press Ltd, *Red Arrows*, IPC Business Press Ltd, 1982.

Lake, Jon (ed), *World Air Power Journal, Volume 22*, Autumn/Fall 1995, Aerospace Publishing Ltd, London, 1995.

Leek, Michael, *Military Low Flying in the UK: The Skill of Pilots and Photographers*, Pen and Sword Books Ltd, 2012.

Lewis, Peter, *The British Bomber since 1914*, 3rd edition, Putnam Aeronautical, London 1980.

——, *The British Bomber since 1912*, 4th edition, Putnam Aeronautical, London, 1979.

Loveless, Anthony, *Red Arrows 1965 Onwards: Inside the RAF's Premier Aerobatic Display Team (Owner's Workshop Manual)*, Haynes Publishing, 2014.

March, Peter R., & Curtis, Howard J., *Military Aircraft Markings 2007*, Midland (Ian Allan Publishing), Hersham, 2007.

March, Peter R. (ed), *The Royal Air Force Yearbook 2009*, RAF Benevolent Fund Enterprises, 2006.

—— (ed), *The Official Royal Air Force Yearbook 2010, 43rd Edition*, The Royal Air Force Charitable Trust Enterprises, Gloucestershire, 2010.

——, *The Red Arrows Story*, The History Press Ltd, 2006.

Having already flown through the valley once, the crew of Hawk Mk132 ZK125, still in yellow primer, decides' the second time around The Mach Loop to take a much wider and higher route in order to have a good look at the photographer. This was taken not far from a location known as Corris Corner. The aircraft was on a test flight from BAE Systems' complex at Warton in Lancashire. *Canon 30D; 400mm, 1/100 sec at f/5.6, ISO 400. (Photo by Graham Farish)*

Above: Of the seventy-five Hawks purchased by Finland, only sixty-seven remained in service in 2013. Of these, forty-one are to be retired by 2016. Those twenty-six aircraft to be kept (one Mk50, seven Mk50A and eighteen Mk66) have been upgraded and are expected to remain in service into the 2030s. One of the lucky survivors, HW-351 Hawk Mk50A of 41 Fighter Squadron (Hävittäjälentolaivue 41 or HävLLv 41) is seen in The Mach Loop in Wales on 4 September 2013 whilst on deployment at RAF Valley. *Canon 7D; 300mm, 1/800 sec at f/5.6, ISO 160. (Photo by Brian Hodgson)*

Opposite Top: Within the deep flowed valley known to aircrews as the A5 Pass, this Hawk T1, XX307, 208 (R) Squadron, negotiates the 70 to 80 degree right-hand bend in spectacular style. Below, and to the right of the photographer, the valley floor drops sharply away a further 91 metres (300 feet), so this pilot has skilfully opted to roll the aircraft almost inverted as he takes the bend, so as to aim the nose of the aircraft in a downward attitude, thereby staying as low as possible once round the corner. This airframe was the 2007 RAF display aircraft and also became the 2009 display aircraft. *Canon 30D; 180mm, 1/640 sec at f/5.0, ISO 200. (Photo by Graham Farish)*

Opposite Bottom: Hawk Mk132 ZK124 is pictured here cruising through the Thirlmere valley in the Lake District in less than ideal weather. This airframe has already been painted in Indian Air Force colours but has had its Indian markings taped-up until it is ready for delivery. It was approximately twelve months later when this aircraft finally got delivered to India. *Canon 30D; 400mm, 1/500 sec at f/5.6, ISO 800. (Photo by Graham Farish)*

— —, *The Red Arrows Story*, (DVD & book pack), The History Press Ltd, 2010.

Mason, Francis K., *The British Fighter since 1912*, Putnam Aeronautical, London, 1993.

McCann, Liam, *Little Book of the RAF – Red Arrows*, G2 Entertainment Ltd, 2012.

Miller, Tim & Gibson, Arthur, *25 Years of the Red Arrows*, Hutchinson, 1990.

Mokwa, Stanislaw Krzysztof, *BAE Hawk T1, Topshots 49*, Kagero, 2010.

Owen, Hilaire, *Creating Top Flight Teams: Unique Team-building Skills from the RAF Red Arrows*, Kogan Page Ltd, 1995.

CPL, *The Red Arrows Magazine*, CPL, 1984.

Reed, Arthur, *BAe Hawk; Modern Combat Aircraft 20*; Ian Allan Ltd, Shepperton, Surrey, 1985.

— —, *Modern Combat Aircraft: British Aerospace Hawk*, Littlehampton Book Services Ltd, 1985.

Robinson, Neil, *On-target Profile No 3: BAE Hawk in Worldwide Service*, The Aviation Workshop, 2003.

The Royal Air Force Handbook, The Definitive MoD Guide, Conway, London, 2006.

Stewart, Andy, *The Red Arrows*, W H Smith Ltd, 1991.

Thetford, Owen, *British Naval Aircraft Since 1912*, 6th edition, Putnam Aeronautical, London, 1982.

— —, *Aircraft of the Royal Air Force Since 1918*, 8th edition, Putnam Aeronautical, London, 1979.

Wheeler, Barry C.,*Military Aircraft Markings & Profiles*, London, 1990.

Wilson, Keith, *Red Arrows in Camera*, J. H. Haynes & Co. Ltd, 2012.

Windle, Dave and Bowman, Martin, *Profiles of Flight; British Aerospace Hawk: Armed Light Attack and Multi-Combat Fighter Trainer*, Pen and Sword Books Ltd, 2010.

Magazines

Ayton, Mark (ed), *AIR International*, Key Publishing Ltd, Stamford, Lincolnshire, various issues, 1972-2007.

Dunnell, Ben (ed), *Aircraft Illustrated*, Ian Allan Publishing Ltd, London, various issues 1974-2007.

Gray, Mike, *Navy News*, Navy Command, HMS Excellent, Portsmouth, various issues 1980-2013.

Green, William & Swanborough, Gordon (eds), *Air Enthusiast*, Key Publishing Ltd, Stamford, Lincolnshire, various issues, 1973-1995.

Hunter, Jamie (ed), *Combat Aircraft,* Key Publishing Ltd, Stamford, Lincolnshire, various issues, 2007-2012.

Morrison, Murdo (ed), *Flight International*, Reed Business Information Ltd, London, various issues 1972-1995.

Warnes, Alan & Parsons, Gary (eds), *Air Forces Monthly*, Key Publishing Ltd, Stamford, Lincolnshire, various issues 2005-2013.

UK Government official and Government sanctioned publications

HM Government, *Securing Britain in an Age of Uncertainty: The Strategic Defence and Security Review*, The Cabinet Office, London, October 2010.

King, P., *Royal Air Force: Aircraft Accident Report: Hawk T1 XX298, 25 October 1984*, Inspectorate of Flight Safety, 1985.

Ministry of Defence, *The Pattern of Military Low Flying Across the United Kingdom 2007-2008, 11th Annual Report by MoD to Parliament*, London, 2009.

Ministry of Defence, *The Pattern of Military Low Flying Across the United Kingdom 2008-2009, 12th Annual Report by MoD to Parliament*, London, 2009.

Stonor, T., *Royal Air Force: Aircraft Accident Report: Hawk T1 XX166, 24 June 1983*, Inspectorate of Flight Safety, 1983.

UK Military Low Flying – An Essential Skill,Ministry of Defence slideshow, London (via the Internet).

Websites *(current as at February 2013)*

It was originally not intended to include a list of aviation websites – official or private – that were consulted (usually for the purposes of confirming the location or serial number of a particular aircraft at a given moment, or to cross-reference a technical point). This was because websites tend to be transient and less permanent than the printed word. Furthermore, many websites are not kept current, including, surprisingly, many official RAF sites (which at the time of writing have proven to be significantly out-of-date, whereas official RN websites tend to be kept current sometimes to within a matter of days). As is already well-known, information on websites can be notoriously unreliable and inaccurate (discrepancies in information even exist between different official RAF sites). However, for the sake of completeness, those websites that have been consulted, even if only cursorily, are listed. It should be noted that some enthusiasts websites require users to register before they are able to access the site.

www.aeronautica.difesa.it
www.armedforces.co.uk/raf/listings/l0027.html
www.aviagraphica.co.uk
aviation-safety.net/wikibase/wiki.php?id=139729
aviation-safety.net/wikibase/wiki.php?id=73567
www.baesystems.com
www.ejection-history.org.uk
www.fightercontrol.co.uk
www.flightglobal.com
www.flickr.com/photos/churchward1956/
www.flylow-flyfast.co.uk
www.globalaviationresource.com/reports/2010/208sqn.php

Another fine photograph of one of the Finnish Air Force Hawk Mk50As, HW-355, that visited RAF Valley for two weeks in September 2013. This was taken from Bluebell, a few miles west of Dinas Mawddwy, within The Mach Loop, on the afternoon of 5 September 2013. *Nikon D300; 300mm, 1/1250 sec at f/4.0, ISO 250. (Photo by Jamie Smith)*

Above: Powering through the long Selkirk to Moffat flowed valley in the Scottish Borders on 23 July 2010, is Hawk T1A XX203, 100 Squadron, RAF Leeming. It was a very welcome sight as this was the only aircraft movement within eight hours of available light whilst on the hillside. Upon closer inspection the back-seater has spotted the photographer and is displaying 'devil horns' with his left hand. *Canon 30D; 300mm, 1/320 sec at f/5.6, ISO 200. (Photo by Graham Farish)*

Opposite Top: This excellent and unusual photograph of a Red Arrow – one of the 'synchro pairs' – low over the sea was taken from the top of Beachy Head in East Sussex on 18 August 2013 when the Red Arrows were performing at the Eastbourne Air Show. *Nikon D300; 300mm, 1/1250 sec at f/5.0, ISO 200. (Photo by Jamie Smith)*

Opposite Bottom: Captured on 4 June 2009 heading through the Cadair Idris pass, this Hawk T1, XX162, of the RAF Centre of Aviation Medicine based at MoD Boscombe Down, is rarely seen in the valleys compared to the regular Hawk T1s from RAF Valley. One of their purposes is the research of how the human body is affected by extreme physical stress from flying fast jets, i.e. severe gravity changes to loss of oxygen from the body (hypoxia). *Canon 30D; 235mm, 1/640 sec at f/6.3, ISO 200. (Photo by Graham Farish)*

www.jmsphotos.co.uk
www.lowflyingphotography.com/
www.lowflymedia.com
www.luftwaffe.de
www.michaelleek.co.uk
www.pb-photos.com
www.projectoceanvision.com/vox-00.htm
www.raf.mod.uk/currentoperations/training.cfm
www.raf.mod.uk/rafvalley
www.raf.mod.uk/rafleeming

www.raf.mod.uk/organisation/boscombedown
www.raf.mod.uk/rafscampton
www.raf.mod.uk/equipment/hawkt1
www.raf.mod.uk/equipment/HawkTMk2
www.raf.mod.uk/reds/
www.rsaf.gov.sa
www.ukserials.com/losses_index.htm
en.wikipedia.org/wiki/BAE_Systems_Hawk
www.7001photography.com

By the same author

The Encyclopaedia of Airbrush Techniques, 1989
The Encyclopaedia of Airbrush Techniques (revised and up-dated), 1990
The Art of Nautical Illustration: A Visual Tribute to the Classic Marine Painters, 1998
Military Low Flying in the United Kingdom: The Skill of Pilots and Photographers, 2012

Contributing author
The New Guide to Illustration, 1990

Assistant editor
Model Shipwright Journal
Shipwright 2012

In preparation
The Panavia Tornado
The British Aerospace Harrier

Unless otherwise stated, the views and opinions expressed in this book are entirely those of the author. They are in no way intended to endorse, reflect, condone or support official UK government, Ministry of Defence (MoD), or BAE Systems practices and policies. They also do not reflect the opinions of the contributors.

The copyright of individual photographs taken by Iain Common, Graham Farish, Brian Hodgson, Alex Klingelhöller, Jamie Smith and Meirion Williams, remain with these contributors, in accordance with the UK Copyright, Designs and Patent Act 1988.

Leading a four-ship, in line ahead, through Glen Tilt in Perthshire, on 10 October 2013 was Hawk T1A XX246, in its special colour scheme. This is based on the Avro Lancaster 'Phantom of the Ruhr' from 1943, to commemorate the ninety-fifth anniversary of 100 Squadron. As will be seen elsewhere in this book, this aircraft, or its partner (two airframes had been painted in this scheme), has been photographed low level in Wales and on the ground at RAF Lossiemouth. It was the first time the author had caught this low level. This aircraft and the three that followed were taking part in Joint Warrior. *Canon 7D; 300mm, 1/640 sec, 1/f9.0, ISO 400. (Photo by Michael Leek)*

Above: Dropping down as it follows the line of the river and just before it has to negotiate the first of a number of very tight bends is Hawk T1A XX200, 100 Squadron. This was taken at the top of Glen Tilt in Perthshire. *Canon 7D; 300mm, 1/640 sec at f/9.0, ISO 400. (Photo by Michael Leek)*

Opposite Top: Passing over Grasmere in the Lake District on 8 August 2008, the MoD Boscombe Down crew of this Hawk T2, ZK010, put the aircraft through its paces. This is one of the earliest flown Hawk T2s that was destined for the RAF and was eventually handed over to 19 (R) Squadron at RAF Valley once testing was complete. *Canon 30D; 400mm, 1/320 sec at f/5.6, ISO 200. (Photo by Graham Farish)*

Opposite Bottom: Having just pulled through Bwlch Oerddrws in mid Wales, Hawk T1, XX335, from 208 (R) Squadron, RAF Valley, banks to port as it heads towards Cad West. This was taken in late autumn, in beautiful light, on the afternoon of 25 November 2008. *Canon 40D; 300mm, 1/500 sec at f/7.1, ISO 400. (Photo by Michael Leek)*

Above: Turning the corner towards Corris in The Mach Loop on 18 July 2007, this Hawk Mk132, ZK125, in yellow primer was subsequently marked up in the colours of the Indian Air Force and then officially handed over to India. A second pass a few minutes later was an added bonus. *Canon 30D; 400mm, 1/1600 sec at f/5.6, ISO 400. (Photo by Graham Farish)*

Opposite Top: In this photograph the graceful lines of the Hawk T1A do not detract from its obvious military purpose as XX200 from 100 Squadron makes an excellent portrait as it powers through Glen Tilt on 10 October 2013. *Canon 7D; 300mm, 1/640 sec at f/9.0, ISO 400. (Photo by Michael Leek)*

Opposite Bottom: Sweeping low through the Thirlmere valley in the Lake District is Hawk Mk132 ZK142 on a test flight from BAE Systems at Warton in Lancashire. This is one of a batch of Hawks that were ordered by the Indian Air Force, with BAe Systems' crews testing each one in different flying roles before delivering them to the Indians. *Canon 30D; 400mm, 1/640 sec at f/7.1, ISO 200. (Photo by Graham Farish)*

Above: The perception of height is emphasized here as this Hawk T1, XX187, from 208 (R) Squadron, seemingly flies along the railway line through the M6 Pass (named after the M6 motorway which also routes through this valley) on 26 August 2010. Some crews take many varied lines of flight through this deceptively narrow looking valley, but this pilot has made every effort to be as low as possible, being a pleasant distance below the photographer's feet and providing a welcome photographic opportunity. *Canon 50D; 300 mm, 1/500 sec at f/7.1, ISO200. (Photo by Graham Farish)*

Opposite Top: A long way from its home at RAF Valley on the Isle of Anglesey in Wales, Hawk T1 XX224, from 208 (R) Squadron, navigates its way through the flowed Selkirk to Moffat valley in the Scottish Borders on 1 March 2010. The snow evident on the hilltops and the cold dry conditions are accentuated by the hot exhaust gases being emitted from the Hawk's engine, which also adds an element of speed to the image. *Canon 30D; 400mm, 1/640 sec at f/6.3, ISO200. (Photo by Graham Farish)*

Opposite Bottom: Pulling out of the Dinas Mawddwy valley on 13 February 2008, Hawk T1 XX167, from 208 (R) Squadron, makes a rapid departure from the low-flying system as the crew climb to several thousand feet for the short journey back to base at RAF Valley as flying at height burns less fuel than down at lower levels. Upon closer inspection the rear crew member has his oxygen mask removed and has his thumb in his mouth, presumably trying to 'pop' his ears to adjust to the difference in pressure as they climb to altitude. *Canon 30D; 300mm, 1/800 sec at f/8, ISO 400. (Photo by Graham Farish)*

The following nine panoramic photographs have been included to show what it's like when British Aerospace Hawk fast-jet trainers are captured approaching the photographer, who has located himself at an appropriate height on a mountainside. Each panoramic photo is an amalgam of up to eight separate frames, then stitched together and edited as a single image. These were all taken within The Mach Loop in mid-Wales (towards the southern edge of the Snowdonia National Park).

The first of these panoramic images was taken on 19 July 2007, and shows six merged images of Hawk T1 XX231, of 208 (R) Squadron, from RAF Valley, Anglesey. (All merged panoramic photos by Michael Leek)

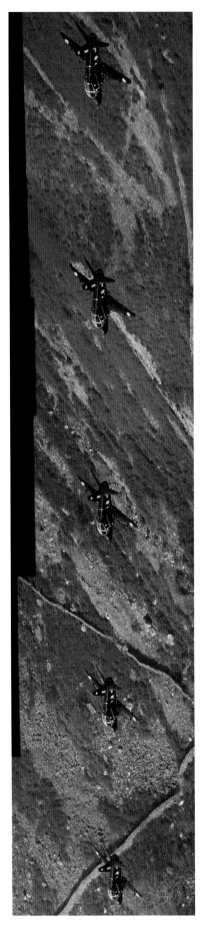

Five merged images of Royal Navy Hawk T1W XX224, from RNAS Culdrose, Cornwall, taken on 24 October 2007.

Eight merged images of an Indian Air Force Hawk Mk 132, from BAE Systems, Warton, Lancashire, taken on 18 July 2007.

Seven merged images of Hawk T1 XX351, 100 Squadron, from RAF Leeming, North Yorkshire, taken on 22 October 2007.

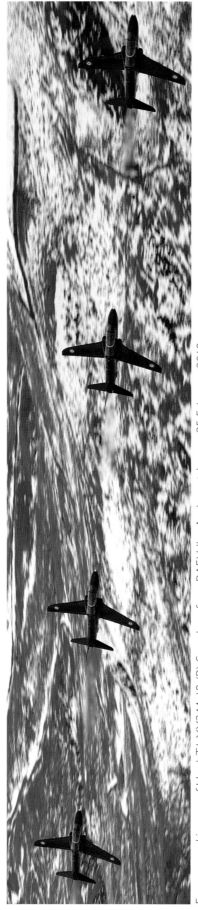

Four merged images of Hawk T1 XX244, 19 (R) Squadron, from RAF Valley, Anglesey, taken on 25 February 2010.

Four merged images of Hawk T1A XX157, 208 (R) Squadron, from RAF Valley, Anglesey, taken on 19 July 2007.

Six merged images of Hawk T1A XX201, 208 (R) Squadron, from RAF Valley, Anglesey, taken on 22 October 2007.

Four merged images of Hawk T1A XX185, 208 (R) Squadron, from RAF Valley, Anglesey, taken on 9 October 2008.

Four merged images of an unidentified Hawk T1, 19 (R) Squadron, from RAF Valley, Anglesey, taken on 22 October 2007.

Index

4 (R) Squadron 86
4 Squadron 134
12 (B) Squadron 22, 34
14 Squadron 40, 100
19 (R) Squadron 12, 15, 24, 44, 68, 82, 84, 96, 100, 107, 114, 129–30, 134, 142, 146, 150, 153, 166, 169–70, 174, 178, 182, 188, 222, 234, 241–2
25 Squadron 124
29 (R) Squadron 22
41 Fighter Squadron 218, 226
43 Squadron 124, 128
54 Squadron 124
56 Squadron 128
63 (R) Squadron 82
74 (R) Squadron 82
74 Squadron 128
79 (R) Squadron 78, 82
79 Squadron 116
87 Squadron 124
92 (R) Squadron 30, 82, 128
100 Squadron 12, 16, 36, 42, 56, 68, 70, 72, 78, 80, 92–3, 99, 102, 104–5, 114, 122, 126, 134, 148, 150, 154, 158, 178, 192, 196, 212, 214, 221, 230, 233–4, 236, 241
101 Squadron 68
111 Squadron 74, 128, 176
151 (R) Squadron 82
151 Squadron 124
208 (R) Squadron 5, 8, 11, 16, 20, 23, 32, 35–6, 40, 48, 51–2, 54–5, 59–60, 64, 70–1, 74–6, 78–80, 82–4, 87, 91–2, 97, 101, 107–11, 117, 125, 130, 133, 137, 141–2, 145, 149–50, 154, 157–8, 166, 170, 173, 177, 181–2, 184, 186, 188, 191–2, 194, 196, 198, 202, 204, 206, 208, 211, 214, 216, 218, 226, 234, 238, 240–2
234 (R) Squadron 78, 82, 216
600 Squadron 124
617 Squadron 22, 72, 160
736 Naval Air Squadron 86, 148
IV (R) Squadron 62, 66, 70, 80, 90, 162, 165, 182, 186, 201, 206, 208
XV (R) Squadron 22, 48, 100, 104

A
A&AEE 42, 82
Aberangell 144
Aden cannon 54, 154, 158, 181
Advanced Stability Training Aircraft 78, 184

aerobatics 98, 105, 120, 122, 124, 128, 132, 136, 140, 152
air 15, 22–3, 28, 30, 36, 47, 55, 64, 70, 74, 78, 84, 97, 128, 138, 141, 148, 152, 156, 160, 176, 180, 190, 202, 210, 212
Airborne Early Warning (AEW) 78
aircraft 5, 8, 10, 14, 16, 20, 22–4, 26, 28, 30, 32, 34, 36, 38–40, 42, 44, 46, 48, 50, 52, 54–6, 58, 60, 62, 66–7, 70, 74, 76, 78–80, 82, 84, 87, 90–2, 97–8, 102–4, 106, 112, 114, 116, 122, 124, 128, 130, 132, 134, 136, 140, 142, 144, 148–50, 152, 154, 160, 162, 168, 170, 172–4, 176, 180, 182, 184, 188, 190, 194, 200–2, 204, 206, 208, 210–12, 218, 220, 222, 224–6, 228, 233–4
  front-line 22, 62, 112
  low-flying 180, 200
  movements 14, 148, 180, 230
  new 38, 66, 128
  operational 22, 58, 62
  stealth 90
  types 22, 68, 152, 172, 224
aircrew 10, 14, 72, 90, 136, 142, 144, 172, 182, 190, 220, 226
airfields 56, 148, 152, 156, 184, 190, 210
airframes 26, 38, 40, 42, 50, 54, 58, 62, 66, 70, 76, 90, 112, 116, 122, 184, 226, 233
Ali Al Salem Air Base 116
altitude 54, 130, 144, 238
amateur photographers 5, 10, 30, 34, 44, 51, 152, 191, 200
Anglesey 5, 82, 86, 128, 142, 144, 148, 240–2
anti-aircraft 42
aperture 172, 176
armed services 14, 78, 112
Armee de l'Air 22
Arrows 7, 14, 19, 26, 28, 34, 38–9, 42, 47, 54, 56, 67–8, 74, 76, 82, 84, 95, 98, 102, 104–5, 118, 124, 128, 132, 136, 138, 140, 160, 188, 224, 228, 230
ASTRA Hawk 78, 82
Austria 98, 122, 138, 190
autofocusing 152, 156, 172, 180
aviation photography 26, 152, 180

B
BAC 111 176
BAE Systems 7, 14, 18, 22, 26, 38, 42, 62, 70, 82, 101, 112, 116, 132, 148, 162, 174, 184, 204, 222, 224–5, 228, 232, 236, 240

Baker, Richard 224
Barker, Flight Lieutenant Matt 74
Battle of Britain Memorial Flight (BBMF) 104
Beard, Wing Commander Dan 62
Bennett, Chris 224
Berlin 158
Bird, Flight Lieutenant Philip 8, 74, 78, 154, 202, 212
Black Arrows 128, 132
Blue Diamonds 128
Bluebell 28, 118, 144, 174, 186, 222, 229
Bowness-on-Windermere 47, 76, 138
Brink Rigg 150
Bristol Britannia 176
Britain 14, 28, 105, 136, 144–5, 148, 152, 156, 178
Brown, Charles E. 164
BushHawk shoulder mount 156, 172
Bwlch Llyn Bach pass 44, 67, 88, 130, 165, 181
Bwlch Oerddrws 5, 8, 15, 23, 27, 64, 68, 75, 79, 84, 91,
    96, 101, 107, 109, 111, 113–14, 117–18, 122, 133, 137,
    144–6, 149–50, 158, 162, 166, 169, 173–4, 177, 184,
    186, 192, 194, 196, 198, 201–2, 204, 212, 216, 218, 234

C
Cad East 8, 71, 96, 101, 144, 170, 188
Cad West 11, 16, 20, 35, 52, 63, 87, 97, 144, 170, 191,
    210, 234
Cadair Idris pass 39, 43–4, 51–2, 71, 83, 87, 94, 96–7,
    107, 110–11, 121, 137, 142, 149, 154, 165, 196, 204,
    208, 214, 230
cameras 10, 28, 42, 44, 51, 74, 102, 106, 132–3, 152, 156,
    160–1, 168, 172, 176, 180, 190, 200, 210–11, 228
    settings 172
Canadian Forces 116
Canon 152, 156, 172, 176, 180, 200, 210
    5D 190
    7D 12, 24, 35, 40, 44, 47, 55, 64, 68, 72, 80, 88, 93, 100,
        102–3, 105–6, 126, 130, 134, 138, 142, 146, 156, 158,
        162, 165–6, 178, 181–2, 184, 188, 190, 192, 198, 201,
        206, 208, 212, 216, 218, 221, 226, 233–4, 236
    10D 84
    20D 36, 68, 206
    30D 20, 56, 76, 122, 142, 158, 172, 174, 182, 196, 202,
        212, 214, 222, 225–6, 230, 234, 236, 238
    40D 5, 8, 11–12, 15–16, 20, 23–4, 27–8, 31–2, 36, 39–
        40, 43–4, 48, 51–2, 56, 60, 63–4, 68, 71–2, 75–6, 79,
        83, 87–8, 91, 93–7, 99, 101, 104–11, 113–14, 117–18,
        121, 125–6, 129, 133–4, 137, 141–2, 145–6, 149–50,
        152–4, 156–7, 161–2, 166, 169–70, 173–4, 178, 184,
        186, 188, 191–2, 194, 196, 198, 202, 204, 206, 208,
        211, 214, 216, 218, 234
    50D 48, 56, 67, 138, 154, 204, 238
    300D 20, 92
    350D 12, 19, 28, 84, 95, 101–2, 104, 118, 184
    450D 92
    A1 176
    AE1 210
    EF 156

EOS 5 180
EOS 7D 156
EOS 10D 180
EOS 40D 152
EOS 350D 152
EOS3 180
T70 180
T90 180
Central Flying School 124, 128, 132
Child, Flight Lieutenant Mike 74, 113, 118, 190
cockpit 46, 54, 62, 112, 158, 184, 201, 214, 220
Cold War 34, 82, 128, 132, 180, 190
colour schemes 36, 50, 66, 76, 102, 128
colours 12, 24, 30, 34, 50, 62, 78, 132, 184, 236
Common, Iain 10, 20, 92, 148, 168, 221, 232
composition 20, 34, 56, 160
Convair C-131 176
Cornwall 15, 42, 86, 88, 103, 240
Corris Corner 59, 144, 225
crews 54, 58, 66, 168, 225, 236, 238
Cunnane, Tony 224
Cunningham, Flight Lieutenant Sean 136, 188
Curtis, Howard J. 224

D
Dassault Falcons 42
Davies, Flight Lieutenant Dave 20, 74, 76, 99, 106, 194,
    214
design 18, 26, 30, 36, 38, 46, 62, 70, 74, 90, 112, 128,
    160, 190, 220
development 26, 30, 116, 220
Dinas Mawddwy 14, 28, 118, 142, 144, 158, 174, 186,
    229, 238
Dissimilar Air Combat Training 42
Dolgellau 14, 142, 144, 149
domestic training 70
Douglas
    DC-3 176
    DC-4 176
    DC-6 176
Duffus Castle 126
Dunsfold 42

E
Eden, Paul 224
Egging, Flight Lieutenant Jon 84, 132, 188
Empire Test Pilots School (ETPS) 42, 78, 82, 184
engine 38, 46, 54, 62, 66, 80, 116, 172, 238
England 6, 14, 30, 42, 82, 134, 144, 148, 168, 206
enthusiasts 18, 26, 30, 34, 42, 56, 74, 144, 148, 152, 174,
    184, 224
exercise 12, 24, 40, 42, 70, 72, 88, 93, 105–6, 128, 134,
    148, 178, 192, 221

F
The Falcons 128
Falkland Islands 22

Farish, Graham 10, 14, 18, 20, 76, 122, 142, 144, 148, 154, 158, 168, 182, 222, 225–6, 230, 232, 234, 236, 238
Farnborough 114, 116, 124, 128
fast-jet
  fighters 62
  pilots 26, 28, 30, 34, 54, 58, 132, 136, 161, 202
  training 22, 34, 38, 46, 54, 62, 74, 78, 87, 112, 130, 132, 145
film 164, 176, 180, 190, 200, 210
Finland 90, 112, 116, 120, 218, 226
Finnish Air Force 66, 90, 116, 120, 218, 229
Finnish Hawks 34, 66, 90, 144
fins 10, 50, 62, 74, 100, 103
First World War 124, 158
Firth of Forth 26
flash units 156
Fleet Requirement and Direction Unit (FRADU) 15, 86
Fleming, Flight Lieutenant Juliette 74, 204
Flieger Revue 190
flight 22, 42, 56, 62, 112, 124, 136, 182, 190, 220, 228, 238
flying 5, 8, 28, 30, 34, 39–40, 42, 50, 54, 66–8, 70, 74, 82, 84, 103, 105, 109, 112, 114, 124, 128, 130, 132, 136, 148, 168, 172, 174, 180, 190, 198, 206, 230, 238
Flying Tigers 128
Flying Training School (FTS) 36, 42, 70, 82, 86, 116, 128, 132, 202
Folland Gnats 38, 42
formation flying 24, 67, 80, 104, 122, 124, 128, 132, 134
France 4, 22, 38, 190, 200
fuel 46, 50, 54, 58, 238
fuselage 11–12, 32, 38, 42, 48, 50, 54, 58, 62, 90, 112, 126, 128, 136, 154, 157, 165

G
Gale, Group Captain Ian 148
Germany 14, 22, 34, 144, 152, 154, 158, 168, 190, 200
Gibson, Arthur 228
Gleave, Wing Commander Christian 70
Glen Tilt 10, 68, 221, 233–4, 236
Gloster Meteor 124
Gnat 38, 128, 132
Goshawk 26, 112, 120
Gough, Jo 74
Griffith, Flight Lieutenant Scott 55, 74, 138
ground crew 14, 72, 90, 136, 140

H
Halina 176
Hanna, Squadron Leader Ray 132, 224
Harrier 10, 26, 54, 62, 70, 74, 86, 112, 125, 134, 182, 232
Hawker Furies 124
Hawker Hunter 26, 30, 38, 112, 128, 190
Hawker Hunters 42
Hawker Siddeley 18, 38, 42, 46, 112, 128
HDR 84, 99, 106, 134, 178
HDR images 24, 32, 35, 93, 95, 106, 126, 134, 141, 160, 178, 198, 218

helicopters 152, 190, 200
Hercules 136, 168
high-gloss finish 91, 148
HMS *Seahawk* 86
Hodgson, Brian 10, 14, 36, 44, 47–8, 55–6, 67–8, 80, 84, 88, 90, 122, 129–30, 134, 138, 144, 148, 158, 165, 174, 176, 181–2, 184, 188, 196, 200–2, 204, 206, 208, 212, 214, 216, 218, 226, 232
Hodson, Gordon 38
Hornets 112
HSA (Hawker Siddeley Aviation) 38
Hunter 30, 38, 128, 191, 200, 224, 228

I
image quality 152, 156
images 10, 14, 20, 23–4, 30, 34, 78, 87, 97, 134, 138, 152, 156, 160, 162, 164, 172, 180, 190, 238, 240–2
Imperial War Museum 106, 200
India 140, 226, 236
Indian Air Force (IAF) 62, 101, 116, 120, 184, 204, 206, 222, 226, 236, 240
Indonesian Air Force 90, 116, 120
instructors 16, 32, 38, 44, 48, 54, 78, 190, 192, 198, 212
Isle of Anglesey 80, 144, 186, 204, 208, 238

J
Jaguar 26, 38, 62
Jet Provost 66, 128, 132
Joint Combat Aircraft 54
JOINT WARRIOR exercises 12, 40, 42, 48, 72, 88, 93, 103, 106, 134, 148, 178, 192, 221, 233
Jupiter Blue Aerobatic Display 120

K
Kay, Andrea 14, 18
Kemble airfield 32, 141
Kenya Air Force 116
King Abdulaziz Air Base 98
Klingelhöller, Alexander 10, 14, 98, 122, 152, 154, 190, 232
Kodak 180
Korea Air Force 120
Kuwait Air Force 116

L
Lake District 148, 180, 182, 188, 208, 214, 222, 226, 234, 236
Lake Windermere 76
Lancashire 14, 82, 101, 148, 176, 184, 222, 225, 236, 240
Lancaster 72, 114, 158, 200, 233
landscape 10, 30, 35, 107, 112, 149, 160, 200, 211
Leek, Michael 5–6, 8, 11–12, 15–16, 19–20, 23–4, 27–8, 31–2, 35–6, 39–40, 43–4, 48, 51–2, 56, 60, 63–4, 68, 71–2, 75–6, 79, 83–4, 87–8, 91, 93–7, 99–111, 113–14, 117–18, 121, 125–6, 130, 133–4, 137, 141–2, 145–6, 149–50, 153–4, 157–8, 161–2, 166, 169–70, 173–4, 178,

184, 186, 188, 190–2, 194, 196, 198, 202, 204, 206, 208, 211, 214, 216, 218, 221, 224, 233–4, 236, 240

lenses 16, 64, 144, 152, 154, 156, 172, 176, 180, 190, 200, 210

light meter 176

Lightnings 22, 26, 48, 50, 54, 62, 70, 90, 112, 128, 172, 176, 200, 220

Lincolnshire 28, 67, 82, 95, 136, 224, 228

locations 10, 12, 14–15, 27, 87, 144, 148, 150, 152, 160, 168–9, 200, 222, 225, 228

Loch Rannoch 10

Loch Tummel 10, 92

London Olympics 74

low-flying photography 10, 12, 34, 52, 79, 97, 148, 152, 156, 169, 172, 174, 200, 210–11

Luftwaffe 22, 28, 154, 232

Lyle, Flight Lieutenant Victoria 66

M

Mach Loop 5, 8, 10–11, 23, 31, 44, 52, 55, 59, 67, 71, 75, 79, 83–4, 87, 94, 108, 110–11, 114, 118, 122, 125, 130, 142, 144, 146, 149, 156–8, 160–2, 165, 169–70, 174, 180–1, 184, 186, 188, 192, 196, 200–2, 204, 206, 210–12, 216, 218, 222, 225–6, 229, 236, 240

Machynlleth 44, 84, 88, 129, 144

Malaysian Air Force 90

manoeuvres 44, 74, 128, 132, 140

markings 20, 32, 71, 103, 134, 154, 162, 165, 182, 186, 201, 204, 206, 224

Marsh, Wing Commander Kevin 62

Martin Baker ejector seat 54, 188

McDonnell-Douglas 112, 210

megapixels 152, 156, 160

Meteors 124, 128, 168

military aircraft 30, 34, 42, 51, 62, 94, 112, 128, 130, 160, 176, 190, 210, 220, 224

missiles 54, 58, 82, 208, 214

missions 78, 158, 190

MoD (Ministry of Defence) 14, 22, 26, 30, 38, 48, 58, 62, 66, 82, 114, 130, 140, 148, 184, 190, 216, 220, 228, 230, 232, 234

monopod 156

Moore, Flight Lieutenant 66, 132, 136

Mosquito 176

mountains 10, 27, 35, 39, 43, 59, 130, 136, 150, 158, 172, 211

N

NATO 12, 22, 42, 78, 116, 128, 134, 148, 178, 190, 220

Navigation Training Unit 70

Netherlands 200

Nikon 28, 59, 76, 88, 114, 118, 156, 174, 177, 182, 186, 194, 200, 202, 204, 208, 210, 212, 222, 229–30

D70 210

D200 177, 204, 210

D300 28, 59, 76, 88, 114, 118, 174, 182, 186, 200, 202, 208, 210, 212, 222, 230

F60 210

Nimrod aircraft 178

No. 3 Flying Training Centre 116

Norway 190, 200

O

Olympus 152

Operation ELLAMY 220

Operation UNIFIED PROTECTOR 220

Owen, Hilaire 228

P

Pentax Z-70 190

Pert, Flight Lieutenant Martin 36, 74, 212

Phantom 30, 158, 168, 200, 210, 233

photographers 10, 20, 30–1, 34–5, 44, 52, 78, 80, 83, 94, 105, 144, 152, 154, 156, 160, 178, 182, 201, 210, 212, 216, 224–6, 230, 232, 240

photographs 8, 14, 18, 23–4, 30, 34, 42, 54, 59, 64, 68, 74, 76, 78–80, 99, 103, 112–14, 118, 136, 142, 144, 148, 150, 152–4, 156, 158, 160, 164, 168, 174, 176, 180, 200, 214, 216, 220–1, 229–30, 232, 236, 240

photography 10, 14, 18, 30, 34, 152, 164, 168, 172, 176, 190, 200, 210, 220

Photomatix Pro 4 160

pilots 11, 16, 20, 24, 26, 28, 30, 34–6, 42, 44, 50, 52, 54–5, 58, 62, 66–7, 70–1, 74, 76, 78, 84, 88, 90, 99, 106, 108, 112–13, 118, 124, 128, 132, 136, 138, 140–2, 154, 161, 168, 173–4, 182, 184, 186, 190–1, 194, 202, 204, 212, 214, 220, 224, 226, 232, 238

Pitlochry 92

processing 152, 156, 160, 164, 180

Q

QFIs (qualified flying instructors) 62, 74, 112, 132, 166

QinetiQ 42

Quwwat 116

R

RAAF (Royal Australian Air Force) 62, 116

RAF 5, 8, 10–12, 14–16, 18–20, 22–4, 26, 28, 30–2, 34, 36, 38–40, 42, 44, 48, 50–2, 54, 56, 58–60, 62–4, 66–8, 70, 72, 74, 76, 78–80, 82, 84, 86–8, 90–3, 95, 99–109, 111–12, 114, 116–18, 121–2, 124–6, 128, 130, 132, 134, 136, 138, 140–2, 144–5, 148–50, 152, 157–8, 162, 166, 168, 172–3, 178, 182, 186, 188, 190–2, 194, 196, 198, 200, 202, 204, 206, 208, 210–12, 214, 216, 218, 220–2, 224, 226, 228–30, 232–4, 238, 240–2

Biggin Hill 128, 132, 190

Boscombe Down 38, 42, 48, 82, 114, 130, 148, 184, 216, 222, 230, 234

Brawdy 42, 78, 82

Brize Norton 68, 136

Chivenor 30, 42, 50, 82

Coningsby 22, 104, 118, 148

Cottesmore 168, 172

Fairford 19, 28, 36, 68, 95, 102, 118, 132, 136, 148, 182, 204

Finningley 56, 70, 82

Greenham Common 132

Hendon 124
Henlow 114
Kemble 136
Lakenheath 10
Leeming 12, 16, 36, 42, 56, 70, 72, 78, 82, 92, 99, 102, 104, 122, 126, 134, 148, 173, 178, 196, 221, 230, 241
Leuchars 22, 28, 36, 74, 78, 95, 105, 108, 128, 134, 148, 178, 194, 196, 214
Lossiemouth 12, 14, 22, 24, 40, 48, 60, 64, 72, 88, 93, 99–100, 102–3, 106, 126, 134, 148, 150, 152, 158, 162, 166, 178, 192, 198, 233
Marham 22, 74, 132, 148, 194
Mildenhall 10
Mona 80
Mount Pleasant 22
North Luffenham 114
Northolt 48, 134, 138
Odiham 152
Scampton 28, 67, 82, 95, 132, 136, 140, 202
Valley 5, 8, 11–12, 15, 23–4, 31–2, 36, 39–40, 42, 44, 51–2, 54, 59, 62–4, 66, 70, 74, 76, 78–80, 82, 84, 86–7, 90–2, 101, 107, 109, 111–12, 114, 118, 121–2, 125, 128, 130, 132, 134, 141–2, 144–5, 148–9, 157, 162, 173, 182, 186, 188, 191, 194, 204, 206, 208, 211–12, 216, 218, 222, 226, 229–30, 234, 238, 240–2
Waddington 100, 148
Wattisham 128
Wyton 56, 82
RAW files 156, 160
Red Arrows 7, 14, 19, 26, 28, 34, 38–9, 42, 47, 54, 56, 67–8, 74, 76, 82, 84, 95, 98, 102, 104–5, 118, 124, 128, 132, 136, 138, 140, 160, 174, 188, 202, 224, 228, 230
Red Pelicans 128, 132
Reed, Arthur 26, 228
resolution 112, 156, 160, 164, 220
RFA Green Rover 42
Riyadh 116
RNAS Culdrose 15, 40, 52, 86, 88, 93, 103, 118, 148, 240
RNAS Yeovilton 86, 88, 148, 184
Rolls-Royce 38, 58, 66
Rosyth 26, 112
Royal Air Force of Oman 90, 116
Royal Australian Air Force (RAAF) 62, 116
Royal Bahraini Air Force 116
Royal Fleet Auxiliary 42
Royal Flying Corps 88, 124
Royal International Air Tattoo (RIAT) 36, 68, 95, 118, 132, 148, 182, 204
Royal Malaysian Air Force 30, 116
Royal Naval Air Station (RNAS) 86
Royal Navy (RN) 22, 26, 30, 40, 42, 52, 54, 78, 80, 88, 90, 103, 108, 112, 116, 125, 136, 154, 186, 190, 208
Royal Navy School of Fighter Control 78
Royal Saudi Air Force (RSAF) 14, 34, 90, 98, 116, 120, 122, 138, 152

S
Sanders, Flight Lieutenant Adam 117
Saunders, Flight Lieutenant 74, 117, 138

Scandinavia 112
Scotland 10, 14, 18, 20, 28, 30, 40, 42, 92, 100, 112, 134, 136, 144, 148, 152, 168, 190, 200
Second World War 22, 50, 72, 78, 104, 114, 124, 158, 176, 178, 190
shutters 76, 152, 156, 158, 169, 172, 176, 180
Sigma 152, 156
Simpson, Duncan 42
skills 10, 14, 67, 112, 124, 128, 136, 140, 176
Smith, Jamie 10, 14, 28, 76, 88, 90, 118, 144, 148, 174, 186, 200, 222, 224, 228–30, 232
Snowdonia 5, 11–12, 16, 20, 43, 71, 111, 121, 129, 136, 202, 206, 210, 240
National Park 12, 43, 121, 129, 202, 206, 210, 240
software 156
Sony 98, 122, 138, 152, 154, 190
sortie 8, 12, 28, 30, 40, 48, 64, 72, 74, 101, 114, 126, 136, 161, 173, 196, 202, 206, 208, 212, 222
South African Air Force 116
Spitfire 12, 104, 200
squadrons 10, 14, 22, 54, 56, 62, 70, 72, 78, 82, 86, 116, 122, 124, 128, 134, 136, 158, 172, 182, 190, 194, 210, 216
Surya Kiran Aerobatic Team 120
Swiss Air Force 120
Switzerland 190

T
T1 7, 11–12, 15–16, 18, 20, 22, 26, 30, 32, 34, 36, 38, 42, 46, 48, 50, 52, 54, 56, 58, 62, 64, 66, 70, 72, 74, 76, 78, 80, 82–4, 87–8, 90–2, 94, 97, 99, 101, 107–9, 112, 114, 116, 118, 121–2, 125, 129–30, 132, 137, 140–2, 144–6, 148–50, 152, 154, 157–8, 165–6, 170, 173, 177, 182, 184, 186, 188, 191–2, 194, 196, 198, 202, 204, 208, 212, 214, 216, 218, 220, 226, 228, 230, 234, 238, 240–2
T1A 7, 26, 31, 36, 38, 40, 42–4, 48, 51, 54–6, 58, 60, 62, 68, 70, 72, 78, 84, 86, 88, 93, 99–100, 102–5, 109–10, 114, 116–18, 122, 126, 129–30, 134, 136, 138, 142, 150, 158, 166, 174, 178, 181, 184, 188, 192, 194, 196, 206, 208, 212, 214, 216, 218, 221, 230, 233–4, 236, 241–2
T1W 59, 71, 96, 111, 129–30, 133–4, 146, 150, 153, 166, 169–70, 196, 198, 211, 214, 240
T2 7–8, 18, 22, 30, 34, 38, 62, 66, 70, 74, 80, 82, 86, 112, 134, 140, 144, 148, 162, 165, 182, 186, 194, 201, 206, 208, 220, 222, 234
T-38 34
T-45 Goshawk 112, 120
Tal-y-Llyn lake 55, 59, 144, 214
Tamron lens 172
Thirlmere Reservoir 16, 56, 122, 148, 150
Tornado 10, 22, 26, 34, 48, 54, 58, 62, 70, 72, 74, 78, 100, 104, 132, 136, 148, 152, 160, 168, 172, 188, 220, 232
training 22, 24, 26, 30, 34, 42, 54, 62, 66, 70, 78, 112, 190, 202, 206
low-flying 35, 54, 71
low-level 34, 44
transparencies 160
tripods 156

Turboméca 38, 58
Typhoons 10, 22, 26, 34, 54, 58, 62, 70, 74, 78, 118, 136, 148, 168, 176, 220

U
undercarriage 32, 50, 54, 56, 112, 176
United Arab Emirates Air Force and Air Defence Hawk Mk 120
United States Marine Corps (USMC) 62, 125
United States Navy (USN) 30, 112, 120
US Eighth Air Force 106
USN Goshawks 26, 112

V
Vampires 124, 128, 168
VC-10 68
Viper 38
Viscount 176
Vulcan 105, 200, 214

W
Wales 5, 8, 10–12, 14–15, 23, 28, 30, 39, 44, 51, 55, 63–4, 67, 71, 78, 80, 82, 84, 86–7, 91, 94, 96, 108–9, 111, 114, 118, 121, 125, 129–30, 136, 144, 148, 156, 165, 169, 174, 180–1, 186, 196, 200, 204, 206, 210, 212, 216, 226, 233–4, 238, 240
Wallington, Flyting Officer Thomas 66
Warsaw Pact 128
warships 42, 78
Warton 14, 18, 62, 82, 101, 148, 184, 204, 222, 225, 236, 240
weapons 20, 24, 34, 38, 42, 50, 54, 58, 62, 66, 72, 78, 112, 190
weather conditions 27, 30, 34–5, 75, 105, 130, 152, 172, 176, 180
Wild, Flying Officer David 66
Williams, Meirion 10, 59, 114, 144, 148, 177, 182, 186, 194, 200, 202, 204, 208, 212, 232
Wiltshire 82, 114
Windermere 47, 138, 148
Windsor Castle 80
wings 50, 58, 62–3, 66, 170, 181, 210

X
XH558 105
XX156 64, 94, 97, 173, 198
XX157 93, 177, 241
XX162 114, 218, 230
XX165 79, 194
XX167 71, 238
XX169 15, 96
XX175 130, 192
XX176 146, 170
XX181 20, 107, 130, 142, 170, 211
XX184 12, 92
XX187 44, 52, 216, 238
XX188 60, 100
XX195 36, 110, 166, 212

XX198 105, 154, 214
XX199 126, 181
XX201 51, 55, 138, 196, 198, 242
XX202 102
XX203 72, 102, 230
XX217 8, 83, 118, 157, 186
XX219 84
XX222 105, 178
XX230 154, 174
XX231 59, 202, 240
XX234 48, 216
XX235 35
XX236 153, 212
XX244 28, 92, 174, 204
XX245 32, 108, 204, 208
XX250 114
XX253 102
XX256 48, 60, 161, 166
XX258 102
XX263 27, 101, 138, 206
XX265 16, 93
XX266 102, 108
XX281 40, 106
XX283 129
XX285 12, 72, 122, 178
XX286 84, 130, 166
XX288 126
XX292 102
XX301 40, 52, 88
XX307 8, 76, 110, 113, 118, 142, 145, 226
XX309 56
XX312 150
XX313 96, 100, 111, 146, 196
XX314 133, 137
XX318 72, 92, 99, 114, 134, 158
XX322 76
XX325 20, 76, 99, 106, 194, 214
XX327 216
XX335 234
XX337 103
XX341 184
XX343 184
XX344 184
XX346 102, 221
XX349 134

Y
Yellowjacks 128, 132

Z
Zeltweg 98, 122, 138
Zenith 176, 180
Zimbabwe Air Force 120
ZK010 80, 186, 206, 208, 222, 234
ZK011 162
ZK024 62, 80
ZK026 80
ZK035 182
ZK121 206